OUR KAT

MEMORIES OF A LOVELY LADY

(In the Rossendale Valley from 1909)

Written from the precious time we spend
together on Saturdays
Going down Memory Lane

Christine

RB

Rossendale Books

Published by Rossendale Books

11 Mowgrain View, Bacup,

Rossendale, Lancashire

OL13 8EJ

England

Published in paperback 2013

Category: Memoirs & Life Story

ISBN : 978-1-291-34651-0

Dedication

To my grandson Roger, who always finds time to phone me every Saturday no matter how busy he is and his two sons my great grandsons Jordan and Adam who always tell me that they love me also Lorna, Roger's wife without Roger's foresight getting me to record my memories, this book would not have existed.

Adam, Lorna, Roger Me and Jordan
On one of their many visits

I would like to say a big thank you to the rest of my grandchildren who are all very special to me.

To my grandson Michael, for all his thoughtfulness and his generosity he as shown me over the years and especially for the surprise gift of my vacuum cleaner.

To my lovely granddaughter Carolyn, who although very busy working as a nurse at Burnley General Hospital and with her own family, my great grandsons Ryan and Jordan and her husband Garry, always makes time to come and visit me.

Also, my granddaughter Lisa who is married to Thomas and lives in Switzerland, her happy phone calls light up my day. Lisa had beautiful twin boys on 7th February 2008 – Mattheo and Elliott.

Finally, yet very important to me, my grandson Christopher of whom I am very proud and of how he has turned out, every Sunday without fail he takes me down to his dad's house and makes me a delicious meal.

OUR KATIE

Family Background

I arrived in this world on 18th January 1909, at number four Robert Street, Piercy, Waterfoot, in the Rossendale Valley this was a typical stone built house in a typical terraced street in Lancashire.
The rain was beating heavily down on the grey stone flags, whilst the wind was howling and blowing a gale it was an extremely cold wet and windy Monday morning, even for the Rossendale Valley, what a stark contrast this was to the inside of our home, in here it was warm and snug with a roaring coal fire burning brightly in the grate, there was joy and happiness at my birth the third child and second daughter of Joseph and Mary Hardman.
I was baptised on the 31st January 1909, at St. Joseph's Church in Stacksteads in the process my Uncle Thomas who was my mother's brother and his wife my Auntie Maggie became my Godparents, they named me Catherine but everybody called me Katie.
My parents were decent honest folk, not rich in the material sense of the word, by any stretch of the imagination, nevertheless, both of them had been born with a high intellect also they had proper moral values and a deep Christian faith, which had been instilled into them from an early age this meant that they stood for no nonsense, we children were expected to abide by and keep the rules. There were

five children in our family, our May was the eldest two years later our Jack was born then me and two years after my birth another boy was born - our Joe – and then last but not least our Margaret.
My mother would lend a hand, helping anyone who was ill or hard up she would tackle anything nothing was too much trouble for her, sometimes she would go to other people's houses and do their washing taking me with her to help turn the big handle on the mangle. Our house was always spick and spam everything had to be perfect, she took great care of things, also my mother could make a nourishing meal out of nothing, there was always good food on the table, she was what people called a clever cook.
I suppose the experiences of her early childhood after her mother had died had left its mark on her, this happened when my mother was just at the tender age of eight, she then had the responsibility of not only looking after herself but had to take care of her younger sister and brother as they travelled around different towns, with their father staying in various lodging houses, while he sought his fortune selling Singer sewing machines, this together with the strength and stamina of her Irish family background all added up to the strong caring capable person she became.

Irish Ancestors

My story starts with my Great Grandfather Andrew Houston and my Great Grandma Bridget O'Boyle. Both of them born in Ireland, Andrew in Erris, County Mayo around 1790, and Bridget in Derryfadda, also in County Mayo in 1818.

The altar in St. Patrick's Church in Lahardane
In the parish of Addergoole

The picture above shows St. Patricks Church in Lahardane, this is where Andrew Houston and Bridget O'Boyle my great grandfather and great grandma got married on 15th October 1840.

Andrew was a writer of verses and songs, which earned him the title of the Nephin Bard he was the first Principal teacher at the Rathkell National School, teaching there from 1844 until 1858, long before the school existed Andrew taught pupils in the hedgerows, he was a famous man in his country a poet and a thinker the people of County Mayo are still singing his songs.

This is the site of the first Rathkell National School built in 1841 in the background you can see the Nephin Mountain.

The Rathkell National School is in the village of Doonbredia, which nestles at the foothills of the Nephin Mountain.

To build the school it cost £99 with additional £7 for furniture, the school was on "Tom Queenan's Hill", on the 31st March 1853, there were 42 boys and 47 girls on the school register, during the year, Andrew and an assistant received a salary of £23.

Andrew and Bridget lived in a house in the field next to the school their four children were born here, the family enjoyed a very happy life in Doonbredia the children attending the Rathkell National School in which their father taught, nevertheless sadly everything was about to change.

Andrew died leaving Bridget with a life-changing decision to make, due to the after effects of the potato famine so many hundreds of Mayo families had followed the migrant path to East Lancashire to find work, and avoided incarceration into the post-famine workhouses in Ireland. So Bridget after her husband's death in 1860, decided to leave the small hamlet of Doonbredia in the village of Lahardane in West Mayo, Ireland, seeking her fortune in England taking with her the four children Ann (16) Cherine (12) Andrew (11 he became my mother's father) and Thomas (9).

After a tiring journey, Bridget and the children arrived in England at Liverpool docks, they eventually ended up in Smallshaw near Rochdale, Lancashire. This is where John Needham his wife their two

children and a lodger lived, how Bridget and the children came to share a four-bedroom house with them is unknown, but the census shows them living here with all their occupations as 'cotton workers' with the exception of Bridget who was listed as 'housekeeper'.
Working in a cotton mill must have come as a great shock to my granddad his brother and his sisters after the free joyous open-air life, all of them had enjoyed in Mayo, but the few pence they earned must have seemed like gold.
There was a cotton mill at Smallshaw a hamlet on the eastern slope of Whitworth Vale, between Rochdale and Rossendale until the mid 20th century, the mill is no longer standing and much of the hamlet has disappeared but Smallshaw Farm, which predates both the mill and the hamlet, is still there.
By 1871, Bridget had moved to Newchurch in Rossendale, residing at Edgeside Holme, the records show her as head of the household with daughter Cherine and sons Andrew and Thomas, sometime before 1881, Bridget went to live with and help Cherine who had married into the Molloy family, unfortunately Cherine had become a widow at the age of thirty-one and was bringing up two small boys aged six and four years old, she named her two sons Andrew and Thomas carrying on the family tradition.

Cherine worked in a mill as a cotton spinner, her brother Thomas who also lived with them was a labourer to a stonemason.
My Great Grandma Bridget died aged 65 on 11th Feb 1883, at Bridleway, Newchurch.
My mother's father Andrew was 23 when he married Catherine Reilly from Newchurch (they named me after her), Andrew and Catherine got married at St. James-the-Less R.C. Church Rawtenstall, on 28th September 1872, they had six children including my mum who was born in 1877, and for around twelve years, they lived in Bridleway, Andrew working in a cotton mill as a spinner.
In 1884, Andrew and Catherine moved to 36 Clement Street, Rochdale, however, within 12 months tragedy had struck - Catherine and three of their children died - leaving Andrew to bring up the other three children Mary (my mum) Annie and Thomas.
After the death of Catherine, Andrew became a commercial traveller, he was the first agent to sell Singer sewing machines, he would take the three children around with him staying in lodgings, by then my mum would have been about eight years old.
Andrew married again on 1st May 1886, to Jessie Sutcliffe who was just 21 years old Jessie was the daughter of Samuel Sutcliffe a Heywood plumber, their marriage took place in St. Stephens Church in Rochdale.

By 1891, they had moved to Chorlton on Medlock, and then something must have happened because seven years later in 1898, Andrew was living by himself in St. Helens, his marriage to Jessie must have ended because he married again on 12th Sept 1898, to Sarah Hutton a St. Helen's widow with four children from her first marriage.

Like his father before him, Andrew was a writer of poems and songs having a book published in 1912, the preface of his book written by Samuel Sutcliffe, Jessie's father describes him as a man who had a well-contented look and a jolly eye and was fond of ease and freedom. From his writings it can be seen that he liked people and liked nothing better than to roam over the moors of the Rossendale area, he had a deep affection for both the Rossendale Valley and his old Irish home in Doonbredia.
He pays tribute to the friendliness of Bacup folk in his poem "Bonny Owd Bacup". His song Molly Magee evokes memories of the summers before the First World War, when the Irish haymakers, experts with scythes and hard workers came over every year to work for the local farmers.

Andrew wrote more than a hundred poems and songs and was a frequent contributor to the columns of leading journals in Liverpool and St. Helens "The Freeman's Journal" and the Rossendale newspapers. More of my Grandad's work, which gained favourable acclaim, was his tribute to *"The Loss of the Titanic"* and *"The Memory of King Edward VII"*.

Andrew might not have been aware about the fourteen young people who left Lahardane, from rural backgrounds, who caught the transatlantic liner from Cobh to the new exciting world of America when he wrote about the loss of the Titanic, although coming from the same area I am sure he would have known some of them. It was with great excitement and anticipation when the young people from Lahardane boarded the fated Titanic at Queenstown on April 10th 1912, eleven of the fourteen Lanardaians perished while three miraculously survived, despite being third class passengers they somehow got into the lifeboats arriving in New York some four to five days later.

The Addergoole Titanic Society, decided to commemorate the sinking of the Titanic and the dreadful loss of so many young lives, by tolling the church bell in St. Patrick's Church in Lahardane, in the parish of Addergoole for half an hour at 2.20 am on 14th April, the exact moment in time when the Titanic sank. The dead of the Titanic may have disappeared into the dark waters of the north Atlantic, but they are remembered by the tolling of a bell at night in the silence and the emptiness across the mountains and plains in West Mayo.

This is the final verse from *The Loss of the Titanic* by my Grandad.

God solace all bereaved ones'
What're their creed or race,
And may His brightest seraphs
Their loved lost friends embrace!
And may the brave who perished,
Be lovingly remember'd
While rolls an ocean wave.

Back to Newchurch in Rossendale

Mary Houston my mum taken around 1895

Eventually, Mary Houston, my mum and her sister Annie made their way back to Newchurch in the Rossendale Valley setting up home there, Thomas their brother went to live in Blackburn with relatives.
My mum had the good fortune to become friends with Grace Redman she lived in Booth with her two brothers the Redman's were quite comfortably off, Grace along with her other friends and my mum used to ride bicycles they were among the first women to do this, being very adventurous women "for this time", they went on long cycle rides which ended up

in places like Malham, Settle, Skipton, Grassington, Whalley, and sometimes even the Lake District.

My mum's sister Annie married Edward Usher, he was a manager at the Co-op, and they went to live in the Co-op house up Weir, my mum's brother Thomas married Maggie Gavaghan and they lived in Waterfoot on Police Row.

My mum married Joseph Hardman, my dad he was a Waterbarner (he came from the area of Waterbarn in Stacksteads), his father John Hardman had been a member of Waterbarn Baptist Chapel, his mother's name before her marriage was Margaret Sweeney she had been born in Prescot in 1856, my Grandma Margaret Hardman had the most amazing blue eyes, almost a violet colour I have never seen anybody else with eyes that colour.
After my Grandfather John Hardman died in 1890, at 35 years of age, my Grandma Hardman had to bring up the children all on her own.

To make some money she took in washing, this would have involved boiling about 2 gallons of water in a big black pan on the fire, when the washing had had a good boiling it was lifted out of the water and put in a dolly tub and rubbed with Dr Lovelace's or carbolic soap then rubbed hard on the ribs of the

rubbing board, it was then possed (twisted and pushed about) by a clothes dolly, this looked like a five-legged dairy stool with a hole in the middle through which there was a handle to twist and turn it then after the washing had been rinsed it needed to be mangled, the mangle was a huge cast iron contraption almost 5' tall with two wooden rollers almost a yard long and 8" in diameter, these were turned by a cast iron wheel at the right hand side about 15" in diameter and connected by large cogs to the rollers.
Then the clothes had to be hung out to dry sometimes the back streets were blocked with the washing on lines, after all that hard work for a family's washing and ironing the payment would only be about six pennies to one shilling, which included fetching and delivery of the load.
My Grandma Hardman worked very hard to bring up her four children Joseph my dad, Jane Alice, John Henry and Ellen (Nellie) they lived on a street with the most wonderful sounding name *'Paradise Street'*, which was in Waterfoot just below Piercy.
My dad being the eldest used to try to help out he would run up Cowpe, with dinners for the workers and earn a few coppers, if he had a spare penny he would go and get some black-eyed peas at the Chip Shop, this gave him an opportunity to read the newspapers there.

It wasn't an easy life, the only light came from gas lamps with mantles, these gave off a poor dim light but most people because they started work at 6 am would go to bed early, when someone wanted to stay in a room, they would light the gas lamps, but if you wanted to move around it had to be either in the semi-dark or use candles lit with matches, most people's eyes got quite used to the dark.
There was always a box of matches and a candle in a candlestick beside the beds at night, although nobody got encouraged to use the candles because of dripping wax over the floor or furniture also the danger of setting light to things.

All the main streets had gas lamps, which were lit each night by a man called a "Lamplighter" he carried a shrouded light on a long pole, which also had a hook on the end to turn the tap on and off. At midnight all the lamps would be turned off.

Bank Street Rawtenstall showing gas lamps

The first supply of Electricity to the town was in 1908. The generating station was at Hareholme Cloughfold.

Picture taken in 1908
My Dad, my sister May, my Mum, and Jack my brother before I was born

After they were married, my mum and dad ran a public house called the Mistletoe, but somehow I do not think this was quite my mum's cup of tea.

Earliest memories

We moved from four Robert Street, into thirty two Booth Road a four-storey house at the bottom of Booth, one of four houses, the toilets were in the cellar, to reach the toilets we had to go down five steep stone steps with no handrail to hold onto.
When it was raining we used to play down there it was a very dark miserable place, when the sun was shining my mum would hang the washing out in front of the cellar door, it used to blow about with a big prop holding the washing line.
The Taylor family lived next door to us and the Barnes and the Peels lived in the other houses.

When our Joe got diphtheria, our May who was aged about 10 years old had to look after Jack and Margaret who was just a baby in a pram, as well as me, because diphtheria was contagious, we could not attend school so we would go up to the fields, which is now Edgeside Park and play all day gathering stones and loads of interesting things, when we saw other children, coming home from school we had to rush and get into the house, then we would quickly run up to the bedroom and empty all sorts of things from our bulging pockets.
In the part of the room were my mum looked after our Joe there was a cotton sheet hung up to keep it separate from the rest of the room.

This must have been a very hard time for my mother, she had no help no nurses or doctors came she had to do everything herself, and I do not know how she kept going, before my mum could be with us she would wash her hands and pull off the pinafore she wore when looking after our Joe, because of the good care my mum took of our Joe, thank goodness he got better and none of us caught diphtheria.

Grace Redman and her two brothers lived in a house behind us on Booth Road, and being Unitarians they had been very kind to my mother when she and Auntie Annie had first arrived in Rossendale, because they did not have any children of their own they made a great fuss of us, In their greenhouse they grew tomatoes, they always gave us plenty of the tomatoes also they gave us homemade buttermilk to drink.

Grace was a caretaker at Waterfoot Council School she would take me with her and let me help with the dusting.

Later on Grace and her brothers went to live in Morecambe and ran a boarding house, when Grace was ready to retire, she asked my mum and dad to go and take it over but my dad wasn't keen on the idea so we stayed in Waterfoot...

Sometimes for our holidays, we would go and stay with my mum's sister Annie and her husband Eddy Usher and their three children Annie, Josie, and Teddy our cousins they lived in the Co-op shop up Weir, my Uncle Eddie was the manager there, we would walk over the tops from Waterfoot to Bacup, playing in the fields on the way, meeting up with them on Bacup Recreation Ground.
We had to wear what clothes we wanted to take we all had two sets of clothes on (we had nothing to carry them in we did not have suitcases then nobody did).
While we were at their home, we had to sleep four in a bed two at the top and two at the bottom.
We always had a great time the grown-ups would relax and chat happily away and put the world to rights, whilst we children had loads of fun running around the fields chasing each other and getting up to all sorts of mischief, when the time came for us to leave there would be lots of goodbyes and hugs and we would set off walking, it always seemed to take us twice as long on the journey back home.

This picture is a wonderful memory of when we met up with our cousins the Ushers on Bacup Recreation Ground

Picture taken on Bacup Recreation Ground

Back row:
Our May, Dad with Joe on his shoulders, Mum, Auntie Annie and Uncle Eddy Usher
Front row:
Annie and Josie Usher, Me, Teddy Usher. (Him and me had just been fighting) and our Jack.

My mum and Auntie Annie Usher used to have lovely hats, which Aunt Jessie (who was the second wife of my Grandad Houston) had brought back from America.

In winter, after it had snowed heavily we always had lots of fun having snowball fights building snowman and sledging, I have very happy memories of this time especially sledging with my brothers Jack and Joe, we would sledge down the big hill from the top of Booth Road (near Fearns Hall) right to the bottom near the shops, our Jack had made the sledge out of a wooden box.

There were plenty of shops at the bottom of Booth, which sold all sorts of things, sometimes our Jack and me use to go to the Co-op at Roebuck, to get other shopping we needed, it was about 15 minutes walk we would set off pulling a trolley, playing counting games on the way there, the trolley was just something else our Jack had made out of a wooden box, and this time had put wheels on.

Our Joe used to say I was bossy but I only wanted to show him the right way to do things.

My father wore a big leather belt, he never ever hit us with it, but the thought of what would happen if we misbehaved was more than enough to stop us.

Shops at the bottom of Booth

One Christmas, Grandma Hardman brought us a big box of chocolates, we did not know what chocolate tasted like we had never eaten it before, we stuffed ourselves and ate every one never having tasted anything so sweet after we had finished every chocolate in the box all of us were very sick!

Farmers with horses and carts would bring fresh vegetables, milk and eggs round to people's houses twice a day early morning and later on in the day.

Elsie Redhead, was a girl whose family worked as farmers, she would help to bring milk round to all the houses, one winters morning as usual she was on her milk round, but unfortunately on that morning there had been an especially severe snowfall, the snow was weighing very heavily on the overhead electric power cable, when her milk cart went underneath the electric cable it touched the big milk churns in her cart! Electrocuting poor Elsie and killing her, what a tragic accident! Something I will never forget.

Lancashire was very honoured when in 1913 we had a visit from Queen Mary and King George V.
We walked over the tops from Booth Road ending up in Cloughfold sitting on a wall, it was very exciting as we watched them travelling up Bacup Road, I can remember waving a flag as they went by in their car.
Everybody who went to school received a cup and a saucer (our Jack gave his to me) to commemorate the day they also got the day off school.

When I started school at St. Peter's, Katy Hatton and Ina O'Donnell became my best friends, Katy's dad Mr. Hatton had come to Rossendale from Staffordshire with five children (their mother had died) he and the children went to live in a big house near St. Anne's Church in Edgeside, Waterfoot.
Ina O'Donnell lived with the McGowan's I know her father was Irish, but we never saw her mother I think her mother must have died as well. Ina was a good-looking girl.

St. Peter's Chapel/School was in a serious state of deterioration and in grave need of a replacement building, so when Bacup and Rawtenstall Grammar School moved from Bridleway to Miller Barn Lane Father Fracassi the priest at St. Joseph's negotiated the purchase of the old grammar school for the sum of £1,100. So that the building could become a church as well as a school, the Rawtenstall Board of Education required alterations, which cost £500 added to this was the cost of £100 for decorating the building, all the fittings had to be brought except the High Altar, which was a gift from St. Marie's Church Bury. Rev. Dean Keighley Parish Priest of St. Marie's Bury performed the Opening and Blessing ceremony on Sunday the 24th December 1916.

At the same time as the purchase of the new premises, St. Peter's was granted Parish status so we could now have baptisms, weddings and funerals at St. Peter's before this we had to go to St. Joseph's in Stacksteads, for anything other than mass on a Sunday.

Father Henry Cashell became the first Parish Priest. Father Cashell was at the parish for five years until his sudden death at Holyhead, after he had decided to take a holiday in his native Cork.

When St. Peter's School moved into the old grammar school in Bridleway, we had to carry all the books over from our old school. For cookery lessons we used to go up to Whitwell Bottom School.

On the 26th September 1916, when I was about seven years old (it was in the middle of the First World War) I just happened to look out of the attic window and saw a German Zeppelin drop a bomb, although I did not know what it was at the time, just a big dark shadow, we had never seen anything other than birds in the sky.
Everybody thought I was making this up until other people said they had seen it, the bomb which was a dummy had been dropped on Heightside House in Newchurch, a police officer carried it all the way to Rawtenstall Police Station, and it is now exhibited in Whittaker Park Museum, Rawtenstall.
At the same time the Germans dropped a bomb up Bacup but they only managed to hit a hen pen nobody was hurt only the poor hens.

My dad's sister Aunt Jane Alice had a very worrying time during the First World War, when My Uncle Mick Meehan her husband had the misfortune to be taken prisoner of war in Poland, besides everything else, it must have been extremely cold there.

Edgeside Hall showing the
Belgian refugees at work

There were quite a lot of Belgian refugees who came to live at the Grand Hall, which was up at the back of what is now Edgeside Park, I volunteered to go up to the Grand Hall collect the Belgian children and take them to St Peter's school.

The Belgian refugees arrived at Rawtenstall railway station in Oct 1914, and stayed until the end of the war, the local farmers and colliers supplied them with free milk and coal.

The Grand Hall had 18 stone-carved faces in pairs on the sides of the windows and inside the main door they included Queen Elizabeth 1, Sir Walter Raleigh,

Queen Victoria and the Prince Consort, Milton and Shakespeare.

The Belgian refugees

The picture shows some of the Belgian children that I used to take to school.

After we made our first Holy Communion at St. Peter's Church, we all went over the road to Father Cashell house for a boiled egg, it was a big house I remember it being very cold, it was in January also it was snowing very hard, and we only had our thin white dresses on, although our Jack was two years older than I was he made his first Holy Communion at the same time.

Our first May Queen was Florie Whitehead, (she later married Wilfred Hatton). Both Katy Hatton and me were very happy when we were told we had been picked to be Maids of Honour, it was very short notice when the teachers told us on the Friday and the procession was due to take place on Sunday, luckily we both had white frocks although we had different coloured shoes, I had black shoes and Katie had brown shoes, we thought this was funny but these were the only shoes that we had, every day we would wear clogs which had wooden soles and leather uppers, we all had one pair of shoes but for best.
When I helped on the allotment at school we were all given packets of seeds and told to dig for victory, and we got to take home the vegetables which we had grown mostly potatoes and Brussels sprouts.
I once went and stayed with the Barons some of my dad’s relatives they lived at Great Harwood, most of the time I was there, I spent in the hen-pen, I thought this was great the hens were so soft and fluffy I could have played in there forever. They had a son who was ordained into the church and later became a Cannon.

The Rossendale Bard
(My Grandad Andrew Houston)

My Grandad Andrew Houston, wrote poems and songs and because of this everybody knew him has the Rossendale Bard he had gone to live in St. Helens, so when he came to visit us at Waterfoot he would come on a train, he was an interesting man so it was very exciting when we went with my mum to the railway station to meet him, as we walked home from the station, we had to walk in a line in front of him and if we did not hold our backs straight he would hit us with his walking stick, he always had this walking stick with him.

We knew all the poems in his book by heart this was just one of them:
Dad

Just a line from father, just a note from Dad,
Wishing you his fond ones, happy times and glad.

Just a Christmas letter, wishing you good cheer,
And a merry yuletide, and a bright new year.

Just a note from father, Con it fondly o'er:
Like the year that's dying soon, he'll be no more.

Kiss the youngsters for him, Romp with them and play
He's with you in the spirit, though he's far away.

Just a note from father wishing you good cheer,
And a jolly Christmas, and a glad new year,

Just a note from Father, neither sad nor glad –
Justa Christmas greeting, justa line from dad.

One Christmas Eve, we were particularly hard up because my dad was ill and had not been able to go to work, Doctor Wilson from Newchurch came to see my dad and realizing we had nothing for Christmas (if you did not work there was no money) he went out and brought some nuts and raisins for us, that is what people did in those days, nobody had much of anything so everyone helped one another whenever they could. The doctor like everybody else had to walk everywhere he always carried a big brown bag.

My grandad wrote this poem on the death of Doctor Robert Wilson, who was a dear old friend.

Tenderly, lovingly, lay him to rest,
Where no harsh winter, blasts shall blow;
And place all around and over his breast
The most tender flowers that grow.
Ah! A genuine friend was he e'er to me,
And a kindly soul to all else was he.
We will miss his genial winning smile,
And his figure so strong and grand,
And the grip of the brawny hand.
Oh! The spirit just gone where pure spirits go
Leaves a void in many hearts here below.
I cannot but drop a tender tear
For the friend of my youth now dead,
And though I'll not follow behind his brier,

Sure, my heart will be there instead.
And with all the fervour within my breast
I will pray for his soul's eternal rest.

The Globe slipper works organised a garden party at Heightside House on Newchurch Road, Katie Hatton and me dressed up as Greek Goddesses, we had loads of fun dancing round the lake we were laughing at each other.

At home, we never had carpets just stone floors, we used to make rag rugs out of any old clothes we had, all our clothes would be handed down until they were well worn and only fit for making rugs all the materials used would be wool or cotton. At weekends we used to have a brass fender with sidepieces on the hearth but these had to go away on Sunday night ready for washday on Monday morning, the water would have splashed all over them, we always had a good coal fire with a boiler at the side that heated up the hot water, for washdays and for bath nights.

Friday night was bath night out would come the tin bath from the back of the cellar door and be placed in front of the coal fire, kettles and saucepans of hot water were used to fill the bath, after all of us had had a hot bath we would sit and have cosy chats in front of the coal fire with a glass of milk.

Lizzie Eastwood used to collect for the church on Friday evenings she would stay and spend some time with us, she later married Bernard one of the Hatton boys.
Before we went to sleep, we used to kneel down by the bed and say our prayers this is a lovely prayer that we all used to say together.

Now I lay me down to sleep,
I pray the Lord my soul to keep;
If I should die before I wake,
I ask the Lord my soul to take.

This hymn by Sister Mary Xavier was one of my favourites

Lord, for tomorrow and its needs
I do not pray;
keep me, my God, from stain of sin
just for today.
Let me both diligently work
and duly pray;
Let me be kind in word and deed,
just for today.
Let me be slow to do my will,
prompt to obey; help me to sacrifice myself,
just for today.
Let me no wrong or idle word unthinking say;
set thou a seal upon my lips just for today.

Let me in season, Lord, be grave, in season gay;
let me be faithful to Thy grace, just for today.
Lord, for tomorrow and its needs
I do not pray;
but keep me, guide me, love me, Lord,
just for today.

By now, I was ten years old and was confirmed at St Peter's Church, this meant among other things that I could take another name I choose Monica.

That is me in the centre on the front row
With my school friends

When our May was 11 years old, she started half time work she would go at 6 am to Hirst's slipper works and then have to attend school in the afternoons.

In the top class at St. Peter's School, there was Katy Hatton, Jack Nightingale and a boy whose father was the stationmaster at Waterfoot railway station and me, it was a real treat when Miss Crook who was one of our teachers she lived in Bury, took the four of us to Salford for a day out and for a special meal.
We always walked everywhere, once when I had a hole in my shoe my dad our Jack our May and myself went on a walk over to Burnley, when we reached Lumb, there was a plague of caterpillars I can still remember the feeling of squelching the caterpillars under my feet!!

My mum had a lot of friends both Catholic and non-Catholic, Rachel Broadhurst was a friend who was the forelady at Hirst's slipper works she would get my mum a big sack of slippers to sew in the evening at home, for a little extra money, when we were in bed we could hear the sewing machine whirring away, I can still remember the sound of that busy machine...

There was a place called the Wood Yard it was at the bottom of Bridleway, many Catholic families used to live in that area, including the Whites the McQuinn's the McGowan's the Moran's and the Swains.

My Grandma Hardman (my dad's mum) had moved from Paradise Street and lived on Bridleway in a back-to-back house, her daughter my Auntie Jane Alice who had married Mick Meehan a big Irish man lived in the other half of the house with their two children Margaret and Fred.

My dad's youngest sister my Auntie Ellen (Nellie) married my mum's cousin Andrew Houston, his dad was my grandad's brother Thomas who had come over with the family from Mayo in 1860.

My Uncle John Henry (my dad's brother) married Phoebe Lee she was a Unitarian and they used to live on Bridleway, in front of their house there was quite a lot of trees which made it very dark inside.

Dickie Debs lived in a big house which he named Ashlands it was in the middle of Turnpike (he made a fortune from felt).

My Uncle Thomas and Auntie Maggie Houston With their four sons, my cousins Andrew, Jimmy, Thomas, and William (Billie)

My Uncle Thomas (my mum's brother) and his wife my Auntie Maggie Houston had four sons they lived on Police Row, which was just off Burnley Road. Tommy Gavaghan, who was my Aunt Maggie's brother had a shop in the middle of Bridleway, I suppose he did well because all the Catholics supported him, the Police Station was also of course on Police Row

My Grandad Andrew Houston died at St. Helens on 13th July 1920.

This was my granddads last poem published in the Rossendale Free Press.

Seventy Today

Come friends less spend one happy day
In Whitewell's lovely dale
And conjure back the cloudless hours
We passed in that clear vale,
Our future meetings must be few
For grieved am I to say
I've heard the Psalmists threescore-ten
I'm seventy today!

Let's toddle up to fair Seat Naze
And view the valley round
Where Rugged moors and frowning rocks
And beauty spots abound
And whilst we listen to the larks
And watch the lambkins play
I'll fancy I'm a stripling still
Though seventy today!

Where now are all our playmates friend?
Gee ! Would it not be fine?
If we'd the power to place them now
Before us in a line
I'd fee as frisky as a colt
As any fawn as gay
I scamper round Cleggs' pasture twice
Though seventy today!

I've had my innings dear old friend,
My battling days are o'er
And Ball and Bat and wicket lad,
Appeal to me no more
For I was born in'49
Upon the first of May
And cannot therefore blink the fact
I'm seventy today!

An obituary published in the Bacup Times on 7th August 1920 read:

Death of Andrew Houston – The Rossendale Bard
He was a frequent contributor to the columns of leading journals in Liverpool and St. Helens and also "The Freemans Journal" and the Rossendale newspapers. His work was published in "100 poems on the European War" and in Forshaw's edition "Pearls of Poetry".

1921 and onwards in Edgeside

We got word that we could have one of the new houses built by the Corporation on Edgeside, I can remember going with my mother to choose which one we wanted we picked 25 Taylor Avenue, which had good views, with nothing built in front of it we could see the hills of Seat Naze, there was a kitchen a living room and three bedrooms also a bathroom with an inside toilet, it was wonderful and better still when we were told we could pick which fireplace we wanted, there was even an inside coal place in those days this was very unusual. So it was in 1921, when I was twelve, we were very thrilled about moving into a brand new house the air of change was all around us but we were still quite unaware about what the future had in store for us, including births, weddings, funerals and thank goodness, we did not know another World War.

My mother gave a warm welcome to everybody the Davidson's became our next-door neighbours, she would help any neighbours, who worked by putting their kettles and dinners on their stoves ready for when they got home, people only had a short time to eat their dinners (there wasn't any work's canteens then), she would go to Mass in the morning and then make dinner every day for many people including Vincent Kilgallen (who later married our May) also our cousins the Ushers.

Sometimes, for dinner it would be potatoes and steak or barley stews or potato pie beside things like oven bottoms and homemade muffins with bacon for the evening meal.
My father with five others helped to set up Hirst's slipper works and understood that he "would be seen all right" but then he became a union representative and of course, this went against him.

Hirst's Machine Room

When I was thirteen years old I started work in Hirst's slipper works, my first job was marking sizes on uppers for shoes, I was quite happy as this was an easy job and the pay was good, my friend Katie's dad Mr. Hatton also worked at Hirst's as a pattern cutter.

On Sundays, we would go to different relatives for tea, Annie Crane a good friend of mine had five aunties they lived in Rawtenstall and Waterfoot, we used to go to each auntie in turn, and then another time we would go to Ina O'Donnell's auntie Mrs. Gallagher people would make us welcome, all though nobody had much of anything we thought it was our duty to go and visit all of them.

Annie Crane's father was killed in a tragic quarry accident, I went to see Annie and stayed at her house trying to help and comfort them as best I could, shortly afterwards, I remember going to Alton Tower Gardens in a taxi with Annie and her mother who was in a wheelchair, her aunties Mary Jane and Polly also her sister Mary they were all dressed in black from top to toe, it was an extremely hot day and I do not know how we all fitted into the taxi.

After this, Annie and her family moved to Rawtenstall but she still carried on working as a weaver at Lolly Mill at the bottom of Bridleway, walking there and back to Rawtenstall every day after a hard day's work in the cotton mill.

St Peter's old Church/School Bridleway Newchurch

St Peter's wanted to buy some land just off Bridleway near to the Mason Arms, to build a new church but the land was found to be sinking.
1924 saw the appointment of Father Francis Magill, a priest who was to have a great effect over the next thirty-three years, Father Magill, soon realised that the Chapel/School had outgrown itself and he set about planning a replacement Church, by ordering the demolition of the original Chapel/School, first used in 1892.

Messer Byron and Noble of Bury designed the new St Peter's Church, twelve months earlier they had designed St Joseph's Church at Stacksteads on a similar style, on 1st October 1927, the corner stone was laid and Dr. Henshaw the Bishop of Salford consecrated the church on 15th July 1928, the cost of the building was £8,300 the altar and the furnishing cost an additional £1,000 there was enough seating for 400 people.

At Easter time we always used to have a passion play at St Peter's, I was once Mary Magdalene and Annie Crane was our Lady and Mary McQuinn was the Angel, in another production I was St. Rose.

Carrying on a tradition, we all helped to scrub St Peter's Church on Good Friday.

There was a family called Boe who came to live on Taylor Avenue, in the Boe family there was quite a lot of children, the mother who was an American was very tall and slim and although she had worked as a nurse in the First World War, because she had not been trained in England, she had to go to Liverpool and retrain before she could be a nurse here, her husband was Irish and he had no idea how to look after the children or run a home, so my mother helped out making meals and making sure the children were all right. I was godmother to Joe Boe, our Margaret and our May became godmothers to other children in the Boe family.

When I was sixteen years old I had a really bad ulcer on my leg it was eating my leg away and I had to stay in bed for sixteen weeks, I was so bored, I started cleaning out the big cupboards on the wall but Dr Persil caught me he swore at me and played heck!! Vincent Kilgallen, who married our May, made me a wireless with valves people called these sets cat's whiskers this really helped to past the time and it was wonderful when Nurse Boe cured my leg by using a dry powder, which no one had even thought about using.

My father suffered from a weak heart, sometimes when he came home at dinnertime from work he would have a slight heart attack, we would have to sit quiet while he came too and then he would get up and go back to work, as well as working at Hirst's he also was the secretary at the Boothfold Working Men's Club, although my dad had not had much education, he was very intelligent good at reckoning up and a beautiful writer with flowing handwriting.

Edgeside Park

When Edgeside Park opened in 1925, it was a good place for people to get together there were benches all along the pathway, every Sunday we would listen to a brass band playing wonderful tunes in the bandstand.

There were amazing tennis courts in the park and Mr. Evans the headmaster at St. Anne's School, Edgeside used to ask me to play tennis with him, I knew how to play tennis having learnt at Bacup Park with my cousins the Ushers, after our game of tennis, we would get a lovely cold drink of water at the drinking fountain.

The children's play area was at the bottom of the park it had a sand pit a shed with benches to sit on three sets of swings a seesaw a roundabout an umbrella and a swinging plank and a big slide.

The bowling green in Edgeside Park

When people played bowls, they got the bowls from the black and white pavilion shown in the picture.

In winter, there was always a game of football going on in a field at the side of the park and then in summer we enjoyed watching cricket matches.

At the back of the park along Edgeside Lane is where a family by the name of Manning lived, Mrs Manning was one of Annie Crane's aunties made lovely pies, and after putting the pies in a big basket, she carried the basket round to all the houses on Edgeside selling her delicious pies. Annie and me used to go round and visit the Manning family to help with the children, when they had a baby who they named Michael, I helped to bath him, the Mannings now have a successful business with cake shops all over Rossendale, little did I know when I was bathing Michael that one day he would become the Mayor of Rawtenstall.

Annie Crane, Gerald Leonard, Eddy Kyle, and me went to Isle of Man for the day, we caught the train at Waterfoot to Liverpool and then the boat to Douglas, it was a shame but on the way over Annie and Gerald became seasick, we just had time for a walk on the prom, we had about an hour there and then we had to come back, on the way back they were seasick again but it had been a great day out for Eddy and me.

When we went on holiday to Blackpool and stayed for a few days, we had to take our own food in a bag this included bread, butter, and a jar of jam, sugar, and tea and eggs with our name marked on them, this was normal, because food was in short supply and guesthouses just did not provide food. Once I went to Blackpool with my cousins the Usher's and we stayed with some relations of theirs who lived in a flat behind the Imperial.

Our Jack, Andrew Houston, Fred Scholes and Jimmy Houston started a band they used to play at St. Peter's school for nothing Jack and Andrew played violins, Fred played the piano and Jimmy the drums.
One week they thought they would make some money for themselves and arranged to play above Spencer's café on Bank Street in Rawtenstall, our Jack and the others worked extremely hard playing all night, Roy Sager who came from Rawtenstall went on the door to collect the entrance money, but at the end of the night there wasn't much money because he had let all his friends in for nothing and this was nearly everybody. I was only allowed to go when Roy Sager said he would keep an eye out for me.

On Sunday evenings we used to go to the Houston's my mum's brother Thomas and his wife Maggie and their four sons, Andrew, Jimmy, Thomas and William (Billie) our cousins for a singsong, they had a piano which Billy Houston played, we all would stand round the piano singing mainly hymns this is what most people used to do for entertainment.
The Houston's opened a Gentlemen's Outfitters shop, which supplied suits to most of the men of Waterfoot.
I was attracted to the Salvation Army and started going to their meetings, when Aunt Maggie made me a bonnet just like the proper uniform ones, it was a lovely surprise.

One Sunday, I went out walking with a lad called Vic Ashworth, he played the piano for the Rossendale Male Voice Choir and the organ at the Unitarian Church, he was supposed to get back and play the organ at a service, but we got back late and so there was no music that evening, his mother came and had a word with me she said "I have nothing against you, you are a very nice girl, but because you are a Catholic it is better that you stop seeing each other" it was a shame but I had to respect her wishes.

I decided along with the Ushers my cousins who lived up Bacup to join the Rossendale Ramblers, we enjoyed going on great walks over the hills and round the countryside in Rossendale we always took a sandwich and a drink with us.
When St. Joseph's in Stacksteads had dances, they played gramophone records, Alice Taylor (she lived behind Houston's shop she was sister to Rachel who lived at Acre Mill, Stacksteads) and me used to dance the Charleston, we would kick our feet out sideways with our knees kept together I don't know how we didn't fall over, it was good fun, we would walk over the Old Road to St. Joseph's and then after dancing all night walk back home.
It was an exciting event, when the Astoria Ballroom first opened on 16th December 1932, there was dancing almost every day of the week with learner's sessions, all Modern sessions an Old Thyme Music Night a 50/50 night and probably the favourite the "Popular" night, which was on Saturdays, as time went on this levelled out and there was dancing on three nights a week. The Astoria was a very special and up market venue for its day being able to boast about 'the purpose made' sprung dance floor, which measured approx 585 sq ft and was covered in maple wood, it was capable of holding a capacity of up to 800 dancers. Annie Durst used to work there in the cloakroom.

Mary Smith was a friend who was a great Ballroom Dancer she used to do exhibition dancing at the Astoria ballroom with Alex Richardson, while I danced with Alex Richardson's friend I loved to dance and wore some lovely dresses, I remember one which was a beautiful shade of green it had a belt with an unusual buckle.

The Catholic Friendly Society would help people when they suffered hard times, my Uncle Andrew Houston and me used to take this money out to deserving people. My Uncle Andrew (he was my mum's cousin) had real sadness in his life, his wife who was my father's sister, Ellen (Nellie) Hardman had died at quite a young age, then Eileen his daughter when she was only fourteen, one cold night after work (she worked in the slipper works), was warming herself in front of the coal fire, still wearing her works pinafore, which was full of solution (glue) when her pinafore caught fire and the fire soon caught hold of her long hair, what a horrific tragedy for someone so young she was burned to death. My mum went to help, but it was too late when she got there, it horrified her when she saw Eileen who looked like a wizen old woman.

Andrew, my Uncle Andrew Houston's son had bad eyesight, I suppose he would have had treatment today, it might have been cataracts, he married one of the Irish girls who came to work at Kearns Mill up Cowpe, and they went to live in Birmingham.
There was about six boys married the Irish girls who came to work at Kearns Mill, beside Andrew Houston there was Joe Connolly, Joe Stinson, Tommy Nolan and one of Wilkinson's.

St John's Ambulance 1934

I became a member of St. Johns Ambulance it was a very proud moment, when we won the cup for the best team in Lancashire we used to do our drill in St. Mary's, Rawtenstall. That is me on the back row second from the right.

When John Henry Hirst's son became twenty-one he paid for every one of his employees, to go to Blackpool for a day out, also we got treated to a meal there were so many of us that we had to go to different hotels for the meal. We caught the train at Waterfoot, it had snowed hard the night before so we were all dressed in wellington boots and warm coats with fur collars, but when we arrived in Blackpool the sun was shining not a spot of snow to be seen we felt very overdressed..

Little did I know how handy it would be in the years to come, when I learnt how to become a dressmaker, going for lessons to a woman who lived at the top of Booth.

I really enjoyed making things and made my mum a beautiful coat, which everybody admired.

Picture shows a tram in Bank Street Rawtenstall

I went to a wedding in Rishton with my Uncle Tommy and Auntie Maggie Houston and their sons Tommy and Billie, Benny Nolan who was a friend of ours, also came with us, the wedding was for a member of the family that my Uncle Tommy Houston used to live with anyway, on the way back coming through Haslingden on the tram Benny Nolan spotted Jenny the girl he later married.
After they got married she opened a dress shop near Stacksteads station.

Katie Hatton married Tom Littler and lived over Stacksteads Old Road, they had a daughter called Anne who married a Norwegian and went to live in Norway.

Ina O'Donnell married Bert Sager and lived in Rawtenstall they had a lovely family (a son and a daughter).

Our May married Vincent Kilgallen and they had one daughter Mary.
Our Jack married Lillian Hall, she was a very good dancing teacher, they had three children Claire, John (I was his godmother) and Peter who how owns and lives on an Orange and Lemon plantation in Almeria, Spain.
Our Joe married Ann Jones who was a lovely looking girl, she had been the Cotton Queen of Ramsbottom, they also had three children, Maureen, Bernice (I was godmother to Bernice) and Michael.
Our Margaret married Harold Bridge they had one son David.

I met my husband John Gordon Walsh, through my cousins the Ushers, his sister Cissy was friendly with them and that was enough to get us talking, we got on straight away, and started seeing each other three times a week with trips to the cinema and long walks when John came to see me he had to walk the 4 miles from Lee Mill to Waterfoot, money was tight in those days, but there was more to do then Waterfoot alone had two cinemas and there were theatres in every town.

John Gordon Walsh

John's grandparents John and Ellen Gordon brought him up and because he was their first grandson, they could not bring themselves to part with him.

John Gordon Walsh in 1911 aged 2 years old

The Gordon's had a big family which included two sets of twins.

There was Polly, then twins Michael and John, Peter (who went to live in Boston, America) Bridget (John's mum) Margaret Ellen (Madge) and the other set of twins, Patrick and Julia and the youngest was Tom.

John and Patrick went to the grammar school everybody else worked in the cotton mills except for John's granddad who was a Blacksmith at Lee Mill Quarry he received his pay in gold sovereigns, he never went out drinking, although sometimes he would enjoy a drink in the house.
All the family played musical instruments and would join up with the Horans (another very musical family) for musical evenings, Patrick used to play the organ at St Josephs Church.
They lived in a big house on Rushton Street at Lee Mill, Stacksteads.

The Gordon Boys - Back row: Patrick and Tom
Front row: Michael, Peter, and John

John with his Uncle John Gordon

This picture is Polly the Gordon's eldest daughter she was born in 1872 she married Mick O'Dea after Polly died he got married again to Biddy Rourke

This is Auntie Madge she was at one time supposed to go and join her brother Peter in Boston, America.

Tom Gordon front row second from right

Tom was the youngest of the Gordon boys this picture was taken when he was in the First World War, Tom fought on the front line and he sent the picture home which was in the form of a postcard with the following message on the back.
"To my dear brother and sister with love
From your loving brother Tom xxx"

John's Mum Bridget Gordon
(Working in the Cotton Mill)

John's dad Joseph Walsh he was a lovely man

After they got married John's mother Bridget Gordon and his father Joseph Walsh, set up home on Dale Street in Bacup, in this house John's younger sisters Mary Ellen (Cissy) and Annie was born.
Dale Street was just a short walk away from Bacup Market, in the market there were many food stalls selling fresh food including fish, it was a bustling place the covered market hall was in an Italian style the grand opening had been in 1867, it contain thirty-nine shops and stalls. Market days were Wednesdays and Saturdays in August there was a Pot Fair, which attracted lots of people.

Inside Bacup Market Hall

Outside stalls on Bacup Market

John as a child predicting winter on the horse and cart from St. Mary's Church the procession is making its way up Rochdale Road in Bacup. Teddy and Josie Usher are also on cart.

When John went to school at St. Mary's Bacup, he would go to his mother's for his dinner but had to walk back to Lee Mill to his grandma and grandad's after school, Mr. Cassidy the schoolteacher used to lodge with his mum and dad and every time John scored a goal for the school football team, Mr. Cassidy gave him a penny.

John on Day trip to Blackpool

The Gordon's ran a very strict household, everybody had to be in by 9 pm but John used to push the boundaries and get home much later, he used to call his grandad the 'Boss'.

We went to stay with John's Uncle Patrick and Auntie Edith in Grantham, Patrick who played the piano extremely well had the bad luck to have his hand shot whilst fighting with the Royal Dublin Fusiliers against the Black and Tans in the First World War, for treatment he eventually ended up in Fernhill Military Hospital, this is where he met Edith she was a nurse there.

Patrick Gordon and Edith Bellamey

John and Me

The picture was taken on our visit to John's Uncle Patrick and Auntie Edith, (I wore the lovely grey dress made of crepe de chine in the picture above).

On one occasion when we stayed in Grantham with Patrick and Edith, we went on a very enjoyable day trip to Skegness, Patrick and Edith had a son called Derek who married Constance she came from Scotland they had three children, Derek is still living in Grantham, and now as quite large family including nine grandchildren.

Day trip to Skegness

John and Me on a day out in Morecambe with Annie John's sister and Bert Lord who became her husband

John and Me in Morecambe

Summer Afternoon in Morecambe

Our Wedding

Finally, after years of saving we could afford our marriage, when we got married, my mother made the food for the reception but many people contributed, I remember Josie Usher my cousin who married Jack Jordan, they lived on Fairfield Avenue, brought a whole side of salmon.

On our wedding day, Emily, Margaret, and Mary McNulty, they lived on Crabtree Avenue brought round to our house a religious picture that they had made with silver paper it was a lovely picture and a nice surprise, and all the better because they had made it themselves. John's Uncle John who was a very quiet well-educated man had been out of work for some time mainly because he was a Catholic and it was very rare to get anything other than manual work however, he got word he had got a job, but had to start on the very day of our wedding it was a shame but he could not come to the do.

We had four bridesmaids, our Margaret, Ann our Joe's wife, Cissy, John's sister and Mary our May's daughter who had just passed for the Grammar School.

The bridesmaids wore lovely long taffeta dresses in a striking shade of rose pink, made by Mary Flannigan who lived at the bottom of Huttockend Lane, Stacksteads, they carried rose pink gladiolas, all the men wore grey suits and carried gloves, I carried a prayer book that Father Magill had given to me which had a cover made of Ivory, Mary Flannigan also made my beautiful wedding dress, my mum purchased her elegant outfit from a shop in Barnoldswick.

Our Wedding Photograph
Everybody looked extremely smart

Our Joe. Cissy (John's sister). Bert Lord (he was married to Annie, John's sister). Mary(our May's daughter). John and me, Dad. Our Margaret, Harold Bridge (who married our Margaret), and Ann (who married our Joe).

After the wedding ceremony at St Peter's Church in Newchurch, we had 'the do' at our home on Taylor Avenue, Edgeside.

The Altar and Sanctuary at St Peter's Church this is where we got married Saturday 24th July 1937.

Informal wedding picture at 25 Taylor Avenue
Auntie Madge is watching out of the window

Annie Crane, got married on the Thursday before us she married Billy Whitehead, I was going to be her bridesmaid but John and me were getting married on the Saturday and because there were such a lot of things I had to do, I was sorry but I just couldn't be her bridesmaid. We were married on Saturday 24th July 1937 July holidays (Wake's Weeks).
After the wedding, we went to Bournemouth on honeymoon, Vincent Kilgallen our May and Mary took us in their car stopping at a few different places on the way, we stayed overnight in Stonehenge, we felt very fortunate as not many people had a car in those days.

There seem to be a great deal of foreign students in Bournemouth nearly every boarding house was full however, after a lot of knocking on doors, thank goodness we eventually managed to find some digs.

John and Me on Honeymoon in Bournemouth

After we were married we lived at Lee Mill, with John's Aunties Madge and Julia and his Uncle John, as their house was quite big we were very grateful that they very kindly let us have the use of the front room and a bedroom.

I was still working going to Hirst's every day catching the bus to Waterfoot and then walking up Burnley Road, to the slipper works, Hirst's was a friendly place to work we used to sing all day long.

The War Years

John was working for the Britannic Insurance Company collecting insurance he had a very good round, when he went on his round up Weir he used to get homemade apple pie with cream given to him. It was a happy day when we managed to get a house to rent on Branch Street, number ten, the Lewis family had the house next door to us.

On 22nd June, we had our first child a girl we called her Joan, I had decided which pram I wanted it was a stylish sleek black one, but John got me a second-hand one it was a big ugly grey thing, it came from Mrs Worsick (they used to have a slipper works) he collected their insurance, I really would have liked to have a nice new pram for my first-born.

Joan and John in the Rose Garden
In Stubbylee Park Bacup

"This Country is at War with Germany"

Winston Churchill relayed this speech to the nation on the 3rd September 1939, shortly after 11.20 am. John along with all the other men got his call up papers and he went into the Royal Artillery.

John in Uniform in the Second World War

There was not much time for training the only training they received was with brush handles at an army barracks in Derby, then he and the rest of his unit found themselves on Hampstead Heath in

London, working on the big guns shooting down German planes.

Anti aircraft guns in action

It must have been a very traumatic time for John when he was loading a big gun on Hampstead Heath and his finger got stuck in the gun, John managed to get some leave and came home for a couple of days, the day he went back the Red Caps arrived at the front door and searched our house, saying he was missing without leave, all Branch Street came out to see what was going on he had stayed a day longer than he should anyway, he must have got back all right, but I did not get any pay for that day.

Our Margaret's husband Harold Bridge was a Royal Marine Commando, he was in Burma during the Second World War they had a very tough time.

My Uncle Andrew Houston's son Thomas fought with the Third Battalion Coldstream Guards in the Second World War, he was only 30 years old when he died on 17th February 1945, his grave is in the Salerno War Cemetery in Italy.

Every person in the country, received a gas mask it was law that everyone had to carry a gas mask with them at all times.
There were not any streetlights, blackout rules were in force (we had to have no lights showing complete blackout) everything was in darkness to break the law was a serious offence it could result in a fine of up to £100 or 3 months in prison, I would walk over the Old Road, with Joan in the pram, to visit my mum at Edgeside and have a meal with her, but always had to get back before the blackout, I would never dare be out after 4 o'clock in the afternoon.
Bombs that should have dropped on Manchester often strayed, this meant the air raid sirens would go off, the sound was deafening, I would take Joan and sit in the small area at the top of the cellar steps, Mrs Lewis next door would sit at the top of her cellar steps, we then communicated by knocking on the

joining wall this was very comforting knowing we were not on our own, both of us scared to death wondering if the bombs would fall on us, this was an extremely terrifying experience.
The Army discharged John because of his bad feet, it was no wonder he had bad feet, the only form of footwear issued had been wellington boots, he went to see Dr. Purcell whose advice was "the best tonic would be to walk on the hills around Stacksteads" when John was feeling better, he managed to get a job in the Bacup Co-op working in the storeroom.

When our second daughter Christine was born on Sunday afternoon on 8th March, it was snowing very hard, and I finally got the pram I wanted, Annie Whitehead gave me a lovely black pram that she had new for her son Thomas who had been born three years before, it was almost like new and it was just what I wanted.

The day my father died, Lillian our Jack's wife who taught dancing had a concert at St Peter's. I went to the concert with Auntie Madge catching the bus for Waterfoot at Stacksteads, when I walked into the hall at St Peter's somehow, I had a feeling that people were staring at me then Judie Manning came over to me and asked "did I not know that my father had dropped dead"? It was such a shock! I rushed out of the hall leaving Auntie Madge there, I ran all the way to my mother's home on Taylor Avenue, Edgeside. My father and our Joe had been to watch a football match at Rossendale, Joe and my dad had parted company at Trickets Wood Yard, Joe going home to his house at the bottom of Cowpe leaving my father to walk home to Taylor Avenue, but he collapsed outside a house on Prospect Terrace, they took him inside and tried to help although nothing could be done to save my dad he had suffered an heart attack and very sadly died. Uncle Andrew Houston had come over from Edgeside on the bus to Stacksteads to tell me the sad news, but our buses had crossed, while I was going to Waterfoot on one bus he was coming the opposite way to Stacksteads on another bus, telephones were unheard of in those days.

We had a grandfather clock, which my dad used to wind up, only my dad could touch the clock after he died the clock stopped working, we never got it going again.

When my father first received his pension which was only 10 shillings a week, it was after all of us had married, he had been putting the money from his pension in those big books we had, shortly after he died my mother found the money when she was cleaning, he hadn't spent it on himself and he hadn't given it to my mother either, she didn't even know it was there but it was a nice surprise.

Christine Me & Joan
The girls are wearing their clogs
Photo taken by our May

We then had a son, our John who was born on 25th March just after he was born we received the news that we had to move out of number ten Branch Street.

Jimmy Woodhouse, who was the owner of both number three and number ten Branch Street, came home from the war, he had been in the Navy and was about to get married, his mother and father had died and his brother was still out fighting in Japan.

He decided he wanted to live in number ten and offered us the house across the street number three so we did not have must choice, it meant we had to flit into three Branch Street, we had to move all his things out from number three then scrub and clean everywhere, before we could move our things in it was in such a state!

The house was full of allsorts and the cellar was full of rubbish, whilst we cleared everything out Jimmy Woodhouse conveniently went out for the day with his girlfriend, I was upset but we could do nothing I just had to get on with it.

We had been very lucky in number ten, it had a hot air oven at the side of the fire which I had used for all the cooking and also the fire heated all the water, we had good neighbours, a young couple Reg and Hannah Barnes lived at number eight and the Wright family had moved into number twelve after the Lewis's flitted.

We had made number ten into a very cosy home, in comparison to the tip in number three there was not even an oven, and the chances of getting one was very slim (there had been no ovens made during the war), with only a little gas jet to do all the cooking on and having to boil the cold water if we needed hot water I felt extremely unhappy.

To top everything John was out of work, making this a particularly hard time for us.

So that we could have a fire in number three, John would take a trolley to the coal store at the end of Booth Road and retrieve bits of coal slack which had fallen out of the coal store, we then mixed the coal with coke to make the fire last longer, coke was cheaper than coal so we would get a bag of coke delivered from the coal man, he would pour this down the cellar from the grate in the street.
One good thing in number three was a large clotheshorse on pulleys, which hung above the fireplace it, was good for airing clothes on after I had ironed them.
In the winter of 1947, John was looking through the daily paper when he saw an advert for a manager in a newspaper shop in Coventry, as things were not very good at this time we had no coal, no money, no heat, and no potatoes we thought we had nothing to lose and answered the advert, we got a reply telling us that John had to meet the owner at Manchester railway station and so that they would recognise each other to wear a rose in his jacket lapel and the shop owner would do the same, the meeting was a success, then the owner wanted to meet me, so John and I went to Coventry on the train just like London, Coventry had been badly bombed in the war there was destruction everywhere.
We were delighted, when the owner offered us the job and it might have been a good move, but Auntie

Madge started crying and Auntie Julie was upset, we just could not go to live in Coventry and leave them.

John, Christine, and Joan
(The girls wore pinafore dresses that I had made using The Gordon's tartan)

Mrs Fenton who was a friend of my mother, sent word she wanted to see me she lived in the Glen in a big house with her husband and daughters Mary, Ella, and Betty, she asked me if I would go to her house twice a week and clean for her, I was very happy to have the job, although there never was much cleaning to do, we used to sit and talk I think she just wanted some company all the family were out at work. Mr. Fenton worked as an industrial chemist and Betty was the head teacher at St. Peter's School. We had a good laugh when she reminded me of the time when Mary, Ella, and Betty were young girls and I had taken them on a walk up Cowpe, all of them wearing lovely white fur muffs, but after playing in the river, the muffs got soaking wet and ended up sort of soggy and grey, I was glad that she saw the funny side.

John eventually got a job as a clicker at Hargreaves and Crowthers slipper works on Rochdale Road, Bacup.

When Joan was about seven after she ate an orange, which had come from St. Vincent's Isle, she became very poorly, also John had tonsillitis and our John was just a baby, Doctor Brookes our family doctor came and sat with Joan and me all night, but she showed no signs of improving so in the morning we had to get an ambulance to take Joan to Fairfield Isolation Hospital, which was just a barn then. Our Joe was living in the Selling-Out Shop (he had a license to sell beers and spirits) at Stacksteads Station, he was the only one with a telephone, so we gave his number to the hospital, later in the day he got a call from the hospital to tell us to get there as quick as we could Joan had got Diphtheria and St. Vincent's disease she was seriously ill and on the free list, today she would have been in intensive care thank goodness Joan started to respond to the treatment.

Because of the war we still had rationing, all Branch Street collected ration coupons to get some chocolate for Joan, but in the hospital some of the patients were German prisoners of war and the nurses who were mainly Irish and should have been neutral decided to give the chocolate to the German prisoners of war!

Branch Street after the War

Nearly everyone who lived on Branch Street was of Irish descent and members of St Joseph's Roman Catholic parish. At one time, the Murrays lived in the Co-op house, we lived at number three, then there was the Wright's next door at number five, when they flitted the Spencer's moved in they had five daughters and their names all began with the letter 'S', at number seven lived Winnie Horan who married Jack Duffy they had one son John, when they moved into the Farholme Tavern the Cook's moved into number seven, Mrs Cook was another of the Horan sisters and had three children Peter, John and Veronica, John married Hilda Murray from the Co-op house. Nearly all the Horan girls when they got married lived on Branch Street. At number nine, although they were no relations to the sisters was a family called Horan they had a son called Jack and a daughter called Dorothy also a spaniel dog by the name of Boots, at number eleven, lived Amy and Elsie Hargreaves and their mother, Tommy and Phyllis Cooper lived at number thirteen a lovely lady they were just a bit better off than most of us, at number fifteen, lived Maggie Horan who had married Mick Grogan they had five children John, Michael, Catherine, Jim, and Margaret, next at number seventeen, lived Mrs Ashworth who was another one of the Horan sisters. She had been a friend of our

May's (May used to go and stay with the Horan's before they all got married) she said they had a most enormous frying pan, in the Ashworth family there were six children Eddy, Mary, Eileen, Sheila, Winifred, and Jim. At number nineteen, there was the Hick's they had a son called Stanley and a daughter whose name was Barbara, Mrs Rawson who lived next to them at number twenty-one was by herself, next, at number twenty-three, was the Calvarery's with their dog Rex and finally at twenty-five, Bridget who was a Horan and had married Matt Connolly - later in life he was the Mayor of Bacup, they had six sons John, Peter, Desmond, Matt, Jim and Brendan and two daughters Mary and Kathleen, the Connolly boys were great singers and good-looking boys.

St Joseph's used to put on very good concerts there nearly always would be a rendering of the lovely Irish song 'Danny Boy' bringing a tear to people's eyes, somebody would recite in Lancashire dialogue, the monologue called Albert and the Lion, which started with 'Thurs a famous seaside place called Blackpool that's noted fur fresh air an fun an Mr and Mrs Ramsbottom went thur with Albert thur son.' Ending with: 'at that Mother got proper blazin an "thank you sir kindly" said she,"What, waste all mi life rearing childer? Tu feed bloody Lions? NOT ME", by the end of the monologue everybody was in fits of laughter.

In the interval you could buy cups of tea with biscuits, then there would be songs like 'My old man said follow the van' with everybody joining in the singing, the evening would end with a rousing rendering of Faith of my Fathers Faith and everybody left for home agreeing what a grand night it had been.

In St Joseph's, school hall on 17th March St Patricks Day, there would always be dancing with a band playing lively music, it was a very friendly night most people we knew were there, I would put green ribbons in the girl's hair, nearly everybody who lived in Branch Street got shamrock sent over from Ireland.

All the children on Branch Street played together the boys played cricket and football. The girls used to skip, they had a skipping rope going across the street with everyone joining in, sometimes there would be two ropes going at the same time, you had to get into the middle and jump over both of them while the girls chanted songs like the "Good ship sailed down the alley, alley ole", the girls also played hopscotch on the flags and they had tops and whips on the tops they drew different chalk markings, which made lovely colourful patterns when whipped, Branch Street was a lively as well as a friendly place to live.

Vera Crisp who lived at the bottom of Huttockend Lane, used to come and play on Branch Street, she had a lovely singing voice the kids would sit on the Co-op steps to listen to her, she would then have a collection charging them a penny each.
In May the girls would get together with their friends and choose a May Queen, they would decorate a pole with crepe paper and have ribbons coming from the top and dress up in their best frocks, the May Queen would sit on a stool and the others would dance around the maypole singing, if they were lucky, people would give them pennies.
In October, the children started to collect wood for the bonfire on 5th November it all got piled into a great mound over the Square, once the bonfire was set alight, we would join all the other neighbours standing around the fire warming ourselves, putting potatoes in the fire to cook until they resembled burnt cinders, then we passed around homemade bonfire toffee. We always had some fireworks to let off, the day before bonfire night there would be great expectation to see which box of fireworks we could afford, John would go and buy a box at the newspaper shop sometimes it would contain Roman Candles, Catherine Wheels, Rockets and Sparklers. Some daring boys over at the bonfire used to let off Bangers and Jumping Jacks behind peoples back, which always made us jump.

At the top of our street, we had a Co-op grocery shop the men who served behind the counter wore long white aprons, nearly all of them had a pencil stub stuck behind their ear, they used the pencil to write down the cost of each item on the wrapping paper then totalled up all the items, they used to weigh the butter out in pats and wrap it in greaseproof paper also grind coffee beans and then put it into bags what lovely aromas there were in that shop, also they cut rashers of bacon on the bacon slicer to what thickness we wanted.

Next-door was the Co-op green grocer who sold fresh fruit and vegetables.

At the top of the next street, we had Webb's bakery and café as well as delicious home baked bread and cakes, they did good dinners, you could either eat in or take a plate get what dinner you wanted and then bring it home to eat, at Easter time there was always a good smell coming from Webb's bakery warm spicy smells, it was all the lovely spices like cinnamon they put into their hot cross buns these were very special I have never tasted any hot cross buns like them since.

Next to Webb's on Newchurch Road just down from Branch Street was Gellibrand's chemist, then a butchers shop, next we had Hartley's chip shop, further down Newchurch Road, Fred Smith had a barbers shop this was next to the Wool Shop I used to buy my Silko bobbins there to use on my sewing machine, then there was Barcroft's grocery shop they were just a bit dearer then the Co-op.

Up Newchurch road, there was Riley's grocery also Heyworth's the Clothes Outfitters, we joined their club this was a good way to save up for things, then still on Newchurch Road there was a paper shop and Barrett's toffee shop, the Farholme Tavern and Laws butchers, across Farholme Lane, there was Mr & Mrs Colbornes grocery shop and Mr Banisters' shop he was a decorator.

Fred Smith Barbers Shop

Mr. Hargreaves had a shoe shop near Stacksteads station this was next to Jenny Nolan's, we took the

children's clogs to get new rubbers on them we also got our shoes soled and heeled there.
We sometimes brought clothes at Jenny Nolan's (who was Benny Nolan's wife) we still had to use clothing coupons, so I made quite a lot of the girls' dresses.

The farmer brought milk round on a horse and cart we would take a jug and get it filled out of his big milk churns.

At the top of Branch Street, there was the Co-op house with a room in which Stacksteads Prize Band used for practising in, we knew Christmas was getting near when we could hear them playing Christmas Carols like. "Adeste fideles, laeti triumphantes, Venite, venite in Bethlehem Natum videtes" this is the Latin version of "O Come all ye Faithful" we still had Mass said in Latin and sang many hymns in Latin.

When Christmas Day arrived after we had been to Mass, I would try to make everything perfect for our Christmas dinner with a lovely white tablecloth the best china and glasses on the table it always looked lovely, John would ask the children if they wanted a shandy and of course they did, somehow he always managed to spill the brown beer all over the clean white tablecloth, we would have a turkey or a capon

ordered from the butchers, I used to make stuffing out of sage and onions we had fresh vegetables roast potatoes, big fat sausages from the butchers and lovely gravy followed by Christmas pudding and custard it was a real feast.
On Christmas day for our tea, we would go to John's mum and dad's John's sister Cissy still lived at home and she would make the tea, she always put on a good spread, John's other sister Annie, her husband Bert and their four children Peter, Barbara, Margaret, and Anne would also be there. The trifle being very special we waited with great anticipation and hoped that the cream, which everybody had a go at whipping would set so that Cissy could spoon it perfectly on top of the fruit, jelly and sponges, when eventually the trifle was ready Cissy would let the delighted children put small silver balls on top of the cream.

We brought a second-hand piano, which we put in the front room, John and Christine had piano lessons from Mr. Cowell who lived on Cemetery Row, we would hear all sorts of music coming from the front room, we kept the front room for special occasions we had our sideboard in there, we got this just after we were married, it had been handmade.
On the floor there was lino, I scrubbed it until it was clean and that's when we discovered there was a

pattern underneath all the dirt, the children loved polishing the floor with Mansion polish pretending to skate with rags tied to their feet, we got a big red and grey rug this brought out the red in the lino and put a nice hearthrug in front of the fireplace, I used to polish the sideboard and the piano, clean the fireplace until it sparkled then I would clean the mirror and the window with Windolene, when we had finished cleaning and polishing the front room shone like a new pin and smelt lovely.
So with a lot of hard work we finally made number three Branch Street into the home we wanted.

We had a wireless which was on hire from the Relay, all of us used to do a lot of reading, getting books from Bacup Library, they had a really good selection also there was a junior section for the children, you could read and listen to the radio at the same time,
Have a Go Joe, with Wilfred Pickles, the Billy Cotton Band Show, Music while you Work, The Archers, Children's Hour, Educating Archie, Life with the Lyons, Overseas Broadcasts to the Forces , The Goon Show, Mrs Dales Diary and Desert Island Discs were just a few of the programmes we used to enjoy.

One thing we had at number three Branch Street was plenty of room, downstairs there was a living room a kitchen, a front room also a long hallway with a vestibule and upstairs two big bedrooms the front bedroom we divided into two rooms, one for a bedroom and had a bathroom put in the other half, there was a big attic and a large cellar.

Because we had so much room, Auntie Madge asked if we would put this couple up from Birmingham, they had started work at Greenbridge Slipper Works with Madge, consequently, Pat James and her husband came to live with us, they had our front room and the attic, but when I think about it why on earth they didn't go and stay with Auntie Madge in the big house at Lee Mill and when I found out that they had relatives in Lee Wood, why they could not have stayed with them I will never know.

The front room came in very handy when our Joe fell on hard times, I was very happy to let our Joe and his family stay, it was a shame but we did not have room for all of them our Joe, Ann, and Michael came to stay with us. Maureen stayed with our Jack and Lillian, Bernice went to stay with our Margaret and Harold who lived with my mum it was very sad their family living apart.

Rossendale Wakes Weeks

To earn extra money, so we could have a holiday John went Union collecting, the last week in July or the first week in August was when we could take our holidays these were Wakes Weeks for the Rossendale Valley, every town in Lancashire had a different two weeks for their holidays.
Wakes Weeks got their name because the entire slipper works, cotton mills and shops closed down for two weeks and buses ran a limited service so people had to take their annual holidays, all at the same time.

Some of the places we stayed at for our holiday were Prestatyn, Llandudno, Whitby, and Grange over Sands, Blackpool, or Morecambe, we were very lucky to have the extra money to afford these holidays as many people 'just used to go for days'.

It came in handy knowing how to make dresses I would always be very busy sewing for a few weeks before we went on holiday, making the girls new clothes to take with us.

John, Joan, Me and Christine at Blackpool

We would catch a coach at Stacksteads Station and when we were going to Blackpool, John used to say to the children the first one to spot Blackpool Tower would get a three-penny bit, so every electric pylon they saw they would shout out they had spotted the Tower.

In Whitby, when we stayed at Mrs Bream's boarding house, which was just opposite the Catholic Church there was a load of steps to climb to get up to the house, Whitby being a busy fishing port meant there were always a lot of seagulls - screeching very loudly flying overhead trying to catch bits of fish especially when the fishermen landed the mornings catch.

Christine, Me and Joan at Whitby

We had to buy our own milk, which we carried from the farm in a kit (an enamel jug with a lid and a carrying handle) we also had to queue up to buy our own bread at the bakers shop. Somehow, a vase got broken so John stuck it back together with glue, Mrs Bream didn't say anything but added it to the bill when we were leaving.

We went to Prestatyn, booking the holiday out of the paper it was staying in a chalet by the sea and it sounded really good, the woman wrote to us saying she would meet us at Prestatyn train station.

Going to the sands at Prestatyn

When the train drew into Prestatyn station on the bridge stood this woman, she was the dirtiest woman I had ever seen, she was waving at the train, I was getting very worried anyway, we got off the train and what a relief this lovely young couple were waiting for us with their car, Mr Brooks and his wife, she was so good looking and smart just like a film star, they took us in their car to this lovely chalet close to the sea and sands, the sun shone every day but the sand which was lovely and soft got very hot because the sand was so hot I burned my feet and they swelled up, however overall we had an enjoyable holiday.

Christine, Me, John and Joan in Morecambe

When we went for a week's holiday to Morecambe our Joan was in the last stages of mumps, fortunately she was over the worse and recovering so she could still enjoy the holiday. We were all very happy because we had found out that summer Joan had passed for Bury Grammar. When our Joan went to Bury Convent Grammar school, she became a very good netball player playing in the school netball team, in the position of goal shooter, she got picked to play for Lancashire and was even asked to have trials for England, but it was going to cost too much money which we didn't have at the time it was a pity but she didn't get to go.

John and Me at Grange over Sands

When we went to Grange over Sands it turned out to be a great holiday we hired a caravan for the week it was in a farmer's field, here it was very quiet and peaceful we walked everywhere, we enjoyed walking into Grange, so that the children could have a swim in the lido (an open air swimming pool) which was right on the sea front, it was a very relaxing holiday.

After Mass on Sunday morning Auntie Madge would call and have a bit of breakfast with us, on Sunday we always had a breakfast of bacon and fried tomatoes and fried bread. Then in the afternoon, if the weather wasn't too bad, we would go for a walk up Farholme Lane then over Stacksteads Recreation Ground and up the cat steps (stone steps in the hillside) from here it was a long steady climb up to Rooley Moor Road, following the road walking for over two hours all the way to Rochdale, it is the highest point in Rossendale at 1555 feet above sea level, on a clear day the views from here are incredible.

The Road over Rooley Moor from Stacksteads to Rochdale

We used to call it the Roman Road, much of the original paving is still there on the road over Rooley Moor and is still in good condition, during the cotton famine of the 1850's and 1860's when there was no work for the poor people of Rossendale, the township employed them to pave the road.

It was a great walk, but we were all very happy when we saw the road leading down into Rochdale and found that the shop that sold drinks and ice cream opened, then we would sit on the wall sharing a drink of lemonade and wait for a bus back to Bacup glad to arrive home, very tired and hungry, but with our lungs full of fresh air.

Other times we would walk up to Stubbylee Park and walk round the Rose gardens and down the Glen this was a magical place with lots of Rhododendron bushes, or we would just sit in the sun and watch the men playing bowls, the children would have a go on the swings and play in the paddling pool and because the base was painted a bright blue, it looked just like the sea.

Another favourite was Maden Recreation Ground we would walk up Fernhill passed Phillips pig farm and over Old Joeys as everybody knew it, then on to the recreation ground here there were swing boats which all the children loved, there was also a shop selling pop and ice cream. This is where my mum my dad my sisters, brothers, and me used to meet up with my Auntie Annie and Uncle Eddy and my cousins the Ushers when I was a child.

When John Maden established Maden Recreation Ground, the official opening being in 1893, it had a lodge a bandstand and a small area of formal grounds, now it is mainly playing fields and the former bandstand and formal garden area are a car park and a children's play area. It is known locally as Bacup Rec. Sir John Henry Maden was a very successful factory owner head of the firm of John Maden & Sons cotton spinners and manufacturers of Bacup, he was also an honorary freeman of Bacup and had been mayor thirteen times in all, eleven times in succession, he served as High Sheriff of Lancashire in 1914, and the following year became a Knight, he was also a Justice of the Peace.

A view over Bacup from Bacup Rec.

It was thundering when John was once walking through Edgeside Park on his way to my mum's house, it then started to lightning the lightning struck John spinning him around and then hurled him to the ground, he was very lucky to be alive, but after this he had a lump appear on the side of his neck, later on the growth turned out to be cancerous, he had to go into Christie's in Manchester and have radium treatment.

What a terrible day I had when I went to see John in Christies, due to a dense thick fog not many people could get to the hospital, even nurses did not turn up, there were hardly any buses running, Billie Mindham who had married Cissy John's sister said he would take me in his car, which was very good of him but I had not bargained for what happened when we got to the hospital, when I got out of the car he drove off leaving me there, after visiting John, I had to make my own way home I managed to get a bus to Haslingden and then had to wait over an hour for a bus to Bacup, when the bus finally arrived I got on and went to pay my fare (I didn't have much money) somehow, there was a foreign coin amongst my money, the bus driver said he could not accept it and that I would have to get off his bus, thank God for the kindly man on the bus who paid my fare. I was extremely worried because I had left Joan, Christine, and John at home hoping to be back a long time before I was finally, I arrived home tired and hungry but could not believe the scene when I opened the door, what a mess, the naughty children had half stripped off the wallpaper in the living room! I was so exhausted I went to bed and cried.

When the hospital sent John home they told him not to get his neck wet, but they sent him out of hospital with radium needles still in his neck, as he didn't have any money for a taxi he caught the bus home it started to pour down with rain and the needles started pinging!! He looked like death warmed up when he finally arrived home.

When our John got fluid on his lungs he was in Birch Hill Hospital near Rochdale for a while, afterwards he went for convalescence to Ormskirk, when he was better we went back to Birch Hill Hospital for a check-up it took three bus changes to get there anyway, we arrived at the clinic and the receptionist asked if we had eaten any dinner to which we replied no, she then told us to wait in this room, after about 15 minutes a nurse came in with two dinners didn't say anything and put the dinners down, we thought that the dinners were for us and tucked in, we had just finished eating when the matron and surgeon came into the room very surprised to see us sat there, it was then we realised that we had eaten their dinners, thank goodness they just laughed.

I decided to have a go at working part time the first job I had was on the late shift at Smith and Nephews wrapping bandages, but that didn't last long, I tried working at Blades Biscuits up Lee Mill, I used to burn my arms taking the trays of biscuits out of the big ovens, but I was able to take home the broken biscuits mainly custard creams this was a bonus. Then I managed to get a part-time job at Birtwistles shoe factory down Farholme Lane, this was more convenient, it was near home and fitted in with school hours John and Christine would come and meet me after school, once whilst they were waiting for me, it was in winter they knocked on a door and started carol singing they didn't see me, it made me mad to think that they were begging for money I banged their heads together.

Every year the Rossendale Boot Shoe and Slipper Operatives Union gave its annual children's treat, because John was a union collector he used to bring home these huge boxes which contained tickets we sorted them out into different areas for about 1,200 children, these had to be given out to the members for their children so that they could get on a free bus, which would take them to the Picture House at Rawtenstall, when the buses arrived at Farholme they would all be full - the children from Bacup would already be on the buses a lot of pushing and shoving and shouting went on but it was a treat not to be missed, each child received sixpence on leaving the cinema after the show, those too young to attend under-fives would be given a shilling and a coloured pencil instead.

The main railway line between Bacup and Bury passed the bottom of our street, it was a great sight to see and to hear the steam locomotives and their accompanying carriages rattling by, we never noticed the noise and the smoke, I suppose we just got used to it, but when the diesel trains began running they were altogether cleaner and quieter everybody commented on the lack of noise.

Mainly just before Whitsun, Joan, Christine and me would catch the train at Stacksteads railway station for Bury then change to the electric train, which went to Manchester there we would buy new coats, hats, and gloves we used to shop mostly at Lewis's department store and at C & A's.

Once a year a circus used to come to Stacksteads Recreation Ground, it transformed the place with a big top tent, which had planks of wood all set round inside for people to sit on, it was a fascinating place for the children with a lion tamer cracking his whip at the lion in a cage, also elephants, and horses which had bareback riders, also tight rope walkers and trapeze artists and lots of clowns throwing water around and of course a Ring Master.

Most Sundays we had a roast dinner with meat and Yorkshire puddings, roast potatoes and vegetables, for tea I would make potato cakes with the left over potatoes, which we had with cold meat from the joint, also salad and then jelly and tin fruit and carnation milk for afters. When we made a jelly for Sunday tea, it would go outside on the kitchen windowsill with a plate on top to stop the birds getting to it. Monday it would be stew made with Sunday's leftover meat nothing was wasted, then on Tuesday, which was the day before payday we would have a large tin of Heinz baked beans with lots of hot buttered toast, every Wednesday (payday), we got our pay packets we would put in our shop order to the Co-op then pick up the box on our way home from work, the children got 4 oz. of sweets between them, which they shared out and they each got a small bar of Cadburys milk tray chocolate this was their ration of toffees for the week, we also allowed them to choose a comic paper Joan picked the School Friend, Christine the Girl and John the Eagle, we would get our dinner from Hartley's chip shop having whatever we fancied, on Thursday I would get some meat at the butchers maybe sausages or chops or liver, to make tasty meals like sausage and mash or liver and onions. Because we did not eat meat on Friday, John used to like a piece of seam tripe for his tea from Hartley's chip shop, while me and the children had a lovely fresh brown loaf, still warm from Webb's with Lancashire crumbly cheese and tomatoes and for a treat a cake of our choice also from Webb's. We didn't own a fridge so the coldest place in the house was at the top of the cellar steps, and here there were shelves to put things on, I remember once that I had saved and brought this large jar of Holicks, but somehow I dropped it and watched it smash all the way down the cellar steps, there was nothing I could do, this really upset me because money was not that easily come by.

Fred Whittaker who lived up Greens and kept hens brought fresh new laid eggs to our house every week, when Fred went to live in New Zealand we missed him. Mrs Wright had moved to Farholme Lane here she had a garden in which she grew rhubarb, sometimes she gave us some of the rhubarb and I would make pies or stewed rhubarb and custard.

Saturday morning, John would go up Bacup to the market and get me potatoes also he called in at the bookies and the library, I would make a potato pie and a winberry or apple pie and rice pudding for dinner and then get the tea ready, usually steak done in the oven with onions, that left Saturday afternoon free, for me to go out and have a look around the shops, which I really enjoyed.

Sometimes on Saturday afternoon, often the girls came with me, we would take the bus to Rawtenstall getting off at Kay Street - on the pavement just at the corner of the cricket ground sat a man with no legs with his cap beside him, it made us realise how lucky we were and we always put a few pennies into his hat - we then continued up Kay Street looking at the lovely shops, then we would walk down Bank Street having a look round Woolworths and maybe calling in at Egan's dress shop, they were friends of our Margaret's it was a bit of an up market shop, we nearly always bumped into somebody I knew (It was a sociable afternoon out) finally, we would arrive at the Market here we would buy Lancashire crumbly cheese and ham off the bone and all things for a salad like tomatoes, lettuce, cress and spring onions and our favourite cake a Battenberg. On the way back we would sometimes call into Fitzpatrick's for a drink this is an original temperance bar, they have served non-alcoholic soft drink beverages since 1890, we enjoyed drinks like dandelion and burdock or sarsaparilla or even black beer and raisin cordial which was a refreshing drink and as been said to help with eyesight and is a great source of vitamin C perfect for boosting your immune system, we had it made with hot water in winter to warm us up.

In summer on Saturday afternoons, John used to go and watch Bacup play cricket, he would follow them to different cricket grounds in towns such as Church, Colne, Rawtenstall, Accrington, Enfield, Haslingden, Rishton and Todmorden, I would go and watch them when they played at home.

It was the time when the legendary Everton Weekes, was the pro for Bacup he scored a century against every other club in the Lancashire League so there was a lot of interesting cricket played, it used to be a good afternoon out, sitting in the sun and enjoying the match watching Everton Weekes, who was a very entertaining cricketer. In one match when he was playing against Rawtenstall, Everton Weekes waited until the ball had passed him, before taking his left hand off his bat and hitting the ball around his back for four.

When the football season began, John loved to watch Bacup Borough play football sometimes taking the children I wasn't very pleased when I found out - I didn't find out until later - that the children used to dodge under the turnstile at the football field to save paying.

After the match was finished they would call in to see John's mum and dad, when the familiar music started about 5 o'clock, everybody had to sit very quiet as the football results were about to come on the radio. John's dad always thought he was going to win the football pools, good or bad, this never happened.

Joseph and Bridget Walsh
Johns Dad and Mum in Blackpool on a day trip

Every week John's mum and dad would go to the Regal Cinema in Bacup to see films such as Meet the Huggets staring Jack Warner as Joe and Kathleen Harrison as Ethel, another favourite was Dixon of Dock Green with Jack Warner as PC George Dixon.

They also loved going to Blackpool for a day out catching the Yellow-Way coach in Bacup centre outside the paper shop, on the way back home the coach would stop at the Tickled Trout Public House known as the halfway house, here you could buy refreshments such as pies and pints of beer.

Mr. Hargreaves who had a shoe shop near Stacksteads Station, supplied ballet and tap shoes for Joan and Christine when they started going to Lillian's (our Jack's wife) dancing class she let them both go and charged just for one of them, Lillian was a great dancing teacher, as well as putting her pupils in for British Ballet Organisation, Tap and National exams she used to put concerts on for charity. As I was good at sewing I use to enjoy making the children's costumes as did all the other mothers.

Christine made a good friend of Maureen Quinn at the dancing class and the friendship as lasted until this day, when they were in their teens they both became professional dancers, Maureen going into the Bluebell Girls and Christine joined the famous John Tiller Girls, (quite a few girls that Lillian taught became professional dancers including Clare (our Jack and Lillian's daughter) Christine Roberts, and Hilary Taylor). Mrs Quinn, Maureen's mother, used to play the piano for the dancing class she was a lovely piano player and could play by ear she only had to listen to a tune then she would play it perfectly.

Lillian used to put shows on at Ross Mill for their Christmas parties, it was lovely that our girls got included when the presents where being given out to the children of people who worked at Ross Mill. We used to have some fun whilst getting ready for the performances.

One of Lillian's Concerts for charity in 1950

When Lillian put a show on at the Mechanics Hall Bacup, there was always a full house - which meant there was lots of money raised for charity.

In June 1953, the Coronation of Queen Elizabeth 11 took place nearly everyone had a street party the whole country joined in the celebration, all the streets around us got together and we all made some food, a lot of organising had gone into making the food but because of the rain we decided to have our party in the tin mission on Holmes Street, in spite of the rain the Coronation of Queen Elizabeth II was certainly a day to remember. An announcement earlier in the year informed us that on June 2nd 1953 at 11 o'clock we would be able to watch the crowning of the Queen on television, however most people who lived around us weren't lucky enough to own a TV set a few that did asked other people in to watch the Coronation, these sets compared to the present day ones were quite primitive the pictures were in black and white and the screens were tiny only 14-inch. Mary our Mays daughter was living in Pimlico just round the corner from Buckingham Palace, so May went down to London to see Mary. They got up very early on the day of the Coronation to get to the Palace before the road was closed off at 5 am, people were sleeping in the streets to get vantage points for viewing the procession, Mary and our May manage to get a good spot at the top of the

Mall near the Palace they were not in the front but the road raised a little giving them a terrific view, they stayed there all day a long day but like the rest of the vast crowd remained cheerful, they saw the procession going to the Abbey there were troupes from all over the world and all kinds of flags, then when the procession returned to the Palace, there was much excitement among the crowds especially for the reappearance of the Queen on the balcony, Mary took many photographs by holding the camera above her head all in black and white.

A typical street party for the Coronation of Queen Elizabeth 11

Also in 1953, Bacup held a carnival with a procession there were floats from every church and works and individual entries all dressed in fancy dress, we managed to get to the top of the street in plenty of time to see it go by. Two big horses with police officers on their backs came into view first, followed by the shiny black official car carrying the Mayor and the Mayoress both were wearing their chains of office, next the Carnival Queen and her attendants smiling and waving, then the Boy Scouts Band playing a good marching tune carrying their banners, then the Morris dancers followed twirling batons in time to the music wearing brightly coloured dresses, next individuals followed on foot dressed in all sorts of costumes including St. Francis of Assisi in his long brown robe a bird perched on his shoulder and a squirrel in his hand, walking next to him was a Pearly King and a Mexican Lady, people were collecting money rattling their boxes, good job we had remembered some change, the Lorries came next shining and sparkling with all the wheels decorated the carpenter had decorated his lorry with beautiful doors and windows, then the coalman's lorry went by, they must have worked hard to get it clean because it was only yesterday the same lorry had been loaded with sacks of coal and here it was displaying a certificate to show that they had won first prize, the lovely bedspreads and curtains displayed on the next lorry showed just what one mill in the district had made, we felt quite proud to be part of a town that could produce shoes and slippers, cotton sheets and pillowcases, curtaining and dress materials to such a high standard... We looked out for people we knew on the Lorries giving them a cheer as they passed by.

A float in Bacup Carnival

The procession ended in Stubblee Park Bacup, in the park there were various stalls games and events, everybody had a good time and thanks goodness the rain had held off.

The Bacup Coconutters

The Bacup Coconutters are unique!
Every Easter Saturday no matter what the weather, they gather at 9 am at the Travellers Rest Public House on Rochdale Road, Bacup accompanied by members of Stacksteads Prize Band to dance their way through the streets calling in every public house on the way, following a tradition that takes them through the town. The music and name of Bacup remains vivid in the memory of people who have seen the Coconutters because nowhere is there a traditional dance team quite like them.
The Coconutters with their blackened faces hats like turbans decorated with a rosette and coloured feathers black jerseys red and white kilts white stockings and shining black Lancashire clogs make a gradely sight. The 'Nut Dance' is unusual and performed in a straight line each dancer wears wooden discs or 'nuts' on his hands knees, and belt.
During the Dance the discs, which are made of maple wood and are struck together in time with the music. The name Coconuts was given to the discs since the

dance came to Lancashire and it is said they resemble the protection to knees and elbows when crawling along narrow seams in the coalmines.
The Garland Dances are performed in square sets; each of the dancers carries an arched Garland decorated with red, white, and blue flowers. These are spring ritual dances connected with the renewal of crops.

One of the Dancers carries a whip and is known as the 'whiffler' or 'whipper in' he precedes the dancers and it is his duty to crack the whip to drive away any evil spirits or forces of evil. The distinctive music is something that you never forget. People lined the streets and waited in anticipation. We always made sure that we got up to the top of the street in time to get a good view catching them when they came out of The Farholme Tavern.

Life starts to change

When John collected union money, one person on his round was a chimney sweep, who lived at the bottom of Huttockend Lane he had purchased a TV and he very kindly said the children could go and watch a programme called Billy Bunter, they were very lucky and really enjoyed this programme, but came home smelling of soot. In 1954, we got our first television we hired it from Relay Vision, when Auntie Madge and Auntie Julia got their first television Julia could not understand it and used to think that the people on the TV could see her. Madge called at our house every night from work she still worked at Greenbridge slipper works, so that by the time she got home, Julia who worked in the cotton mill at Acre Mill had made the fire, later on to stop all the falling out John went up to Lee Mill every evening to bring the coal up from the cellar for their fire as they never gave him a key he would be outside in all weathers banging on the window to get in. Madge was a very strong willed woman if she saw any cat outside she would open the first door she came to and put the cat into the house even if it didn't belong there. Julia who was a very smartly dressed woman started behaving strangely she would go outside at night in her nightdress and bang on peoples cars, so the decision was made that she would have to go into Moorlands (Rossendale General Hospital), I took her with her packed suitcase anyway the doctor sat her down and asked her questions about everyday things like who was the Prime Minister, it was unbelievable she answered everything correctly he said to me "what have you brought her here for and what is that suitcase for there is nothing wrong with this woman, take her and the suitcase home" I felt terrible. Our Joan used to go up to Lee Mill on a Saturday morning taking Madge and Julia's bread up from Webb's and do other errands for things they needed.

On my mother's eightieth birthday we had a family party at our house we blew up balloons and put up paper streamers, I made a big potato pie in two big washing up bowls, all my sisters and brothers and their children came we had a lovely time everybody had to do a party piece, I was just sorry that when Ann our Joe's wife arrived there was no potato pie left, she had to work that day (she was the cook at Loveclough print works) I had put some potato pie on one side for her but somebody had eaten it.

May, Me, Mum, Jack, Margaret and Joe at the party we had at our house for my mum's 80th birthday - February 1957

I was working part time at Birtwistles Slipper Works down Farholme Lane and managed to get our Joe a job there, he used to come home with me at dinnertime, sometimes I would leave a pan of stew on the stove on a low light because we didn't have that much time.

We could see the railway line from Birtwistles Slipper Works, I remember the day that our Joe's daughter Maureen was going to live in Canada and get married to Norman a Canadian she had met at the Astoria,

Joe and I stood waving out of the factory window we could see Maureen waving to us on the train she had got on at Bacup station I remember thinking how brave to be going all that way by herself.

She married Norman on Vancouver Island, they had three children Paul, Michael and Barbara (Barbara was born on my birthday 18th January) later on they all went to live in America the children are now grown-up and have families themselves. Maureen told me on one of her visits back here that when she was leaving the docks at Liverpool on her way to live in Canada, she wondered what thoughts Andrew Houston her great granddad would have had when he arrived with his mother, sisters and brother from Ireland at the very same docks in 1860. Sadly, after nearly 50 happy years of marriage Norman died on Thursday, August 20, 2005, he was a wonderful man and touched many lives however Maureen is still enjoying life in Florida she always knew what she wanted.

It was one of the saddest days of my life when my mother died of bowel cancer when she was eighty-three, once she became ill we all thought it best if she came and lived with me so that I could look after her, I gave up work (I was only working part-time) this meant I had more time to give my mum the care and attention she needed we put her bed in the front room and we had keys cut for Jack, May, Joe, and Margaret to use the front door so that they could visit my mum anytime they wanted. Our Jack didn't say anything to anybody but always gave me a shilling or two to help. The district nurse came and saw my mum everyday but not much could be done to help her, it was a very heart breaking time when my mum stopped eating she would not take any food from me, I think she thought I had put poison in the food I tried getting the girls to take the food into her but she still would not eat it, one thing I regret was the firm I got to supply and laundered sheets the sheets they sent us turned out to be of an extremely rough texture. When my mother died there was a great void in my life, as well as being a strong woman, she had always been a warm, gentle and caring person also understanding and very wise.

I knew that I had lost someone very special and I missed her every day.

In 1961 our May with her daughter Mary and Mary's husband Eric and their two children Andy and Patricia emigrated they went on the £10 scheme to Australia on the P. & O. Liner Strathmore, during the war, it had served as a troop ship Harold Bridge our Margaret's husband who was a Royal Marine had gone on the same ship to Burma. The Strathmore was travelling round the world as a cruise ship stopping at famous ports in the Mediterranean they stayed overnight in Egypt and India and were able to go ashore, May had a lovely time on the way over somehow she travelled first class and got to meet the victorious Australian cricket team, they were taking the "Ashes" back to Australia, May and Mary got all their autographs. When they arrived in Australia the migrant hostel at 'Fairy Meadow' contrasted badly with the grand voyage, at first they had a rough time, Mary was pregnant with Meryl and Eric her husband broke his ankle, but they survived and things got better, after five weeks at Fairy Meadow they moved to a house near the beach at Warilla, Meryl was born here on 18th January my birthday. I know May was undecided about whether to go, but she made the right choice and was able to help with the children, when Mary continued her career as an art teacher. Our May had 15 good years there making many friends before sadly she died, our Margaret sent May the Rossendale Free Press newspaper, which she enjoyed and kept her up to date with what was happening here. Mary as made a great life for herself and to say she was an only child her family is quite large now including four great grandchildren.

When our first grandson Michael, was born to our Christine, who was living in Norwood Junction, London it had been the worst winter for a long time, I travelled down to see them catching a National Express Coach from Manchester, the weather was terrible it was snowing very hard we were only halfway there when the driver had to change the wheels on the coach, eventually the coach arrived at Victoria coach station, I then had to get to Victoria railway station (I wasn't used to London) and catch a train to Norwood Junction, but there is also a station at Norwood, I made a bad mistake and got off at the wrong station, by the time the right train came it was late evening, when I finally arrived in Norwood

Junction it was very dark, thank goodness, I knew there was a red phone box at the top of the road because Christine used to ring us from there, so I managed to find Albert Road and knowing what colour curtains she had, because I had made them for her, at last feeling very cold and weary I managed to find their flat. Never have I been so glad to find anywhere, but after seeing what a perfect baby Michael was I soon forgot my ordeal.

By the time, Roger was born Christine's second son they had moved back to Lancashire living up Bacup and because we lived quite near I was able to help. Auntie Madge and Julia loved looking after the boys and used to try to outdo each other and be the first one to get to their house on a Tuesday, so that Christine could go to the Post Office and collect the family allowance of eight shillings, which you got if you had two children.

I started working at Kilnhome Slipper Works and I stayed there until I retired, after retiring I got a pension of 20 pence a week, which I used to leave until I had a pound it was just enough to pay my bus fare to Rawtenstall.

Our Joan give birth to Carolyn our first granddaughter and then two years after Lisa was born the day before John's birthday, so we now had four grandchildren, two boys and two beautiful girls our family was growing.

Sadly in 1970, Julia died and then two years later Madge died, it was very heartbreaking after Madge had died John and I had to clear out Lee Mill house and it was then that we found this trunk, it was full of rolls of material also new things that Madge had brought to take with her when she was going to live with her brother Peter in Boston America, but for some reason when she didn't go - we never knew why she never talked about it - the trunk had remained untouched.

Life after Branch Street

When I retired from work, we sold three Branch Street after advertising it for sale in the Manchester Evening News, and we brought this cosy house with a landing and a garden on Kiln Terrace this was a much smaller house it was what is known as a back-to-back, and because the landing caught the sun all day long John called it Costa Landing it was a welcoming home with a lovely warm feeling in summer the sun shone directly into the sitting room, Kiln Terrace was in a convenient place - the bus stop for Rawtenstall was just at the front of our house on Newchurch Road and the bus stop for Bacup was across the road this was very handy, also nearby in walking distance there were quite a few shops.

We were fortunate in having good neighbours on one side of us were Ian, Joan, and their three children on the other the doctor's surgery, at the front of us lived Floe and Jack on Newchurch Road their door opened out onto the main road they had no sun at all and nowhere to sit out, so when they asked if they could come and sit in our garden we didn't mind at all they really enjoyed sitting in the sunshine. Mabel who lived at the other side of the landing became quite a good friend and at the far end of the landing lived Jan who had quads she was very generous, if she saw John going to Bacup on the bus she would always pay his fare.

One day I was in severe pain with arthritis so I went to the doctors for some tablets, when I got home I went straight upstairs for a lay down and saw what I thought was John's green tie on the floor bent down to pick it up but to my horror! I couldn't believe it - it wasn't a tie but a snake! I dropped it very quickly, the snake's mouth kept opening and shutting with its tongue going in and out, I was stunned I shouted out for John to come and help with the snake but he didn't take much notice he thought I was hallucinating, finally he came up to the bedroom and realizing there definitely was a snake went downstairs to get a shovel and managed to get the snake onto the shovel and thank goodness get the snake out of the house, it turned out that the snake was a pet and belonged to the little boy who lived in the flat above the doctors. Afterwards everybody had a good laugh at my expense and the snake was christened Hissing Sid.

When the doctor's surgery became a flat we got more good neighbours: Bob and Lorraine.

We were delighted when in March 1981, our John and his wife Emily had a son, Christopher another grandson for us...

Lisa our Joan's daughter was a great swimmer especially when she swum butterfly stroke, we used to go and watch her in Galas at Bacup Baths, Annie and Harry, Roy's mum and dad (our Joan's husband) would go to watch as well we were all very proud of our granddaughter Lisa used to win every race, it was very exciting when in one event she was the last swimmer in a relay race, her team was losing, but she made up the distance and when her team won the crowds were going wild cheering. She represented Great Britain swimming in a few different countries including Spain and Ireland, a lot of training went into being such a good swimmer - before school Lisa and her dad would travel to baths, which were the right length for training.

After John retired from the slipper works, he got a job at Nat West Bank as a security guard, he would help the girls in the bank to balance the day's takings (he was very good with figures) John then took the money from the Stacksteads branch up to the main bank in Bacup, because we didn't have a car he had to go on the bus sometimes he would have a lot of money to carry.

When he was 70 he retired from the bank, he then got a part-time job at the Bookies, which he really enjoyed also on Saturdays John helped Christine out with her bookstall on Rawtenstall Market, he liked to keep busy, he was always doing crosswords and won £50 doing the crossword in the News of the World a few times, John also won £5 and had the following story published in a magazine called "Irelands Own".

PHEW

There was a family of skunks, Ma and Pa
And two little ones called In and Out.
Wherever Out went, In was sure to be with him,
Until one day, Out came back alone.
"Where's In?" said Ma. "I have lost him", said Out.
"Well", said Ma, "go and look for him
And do not come back 'till you have found him".
About a week later Out came back with In.
"You clever little skunk", said Ma.
"How and where did you find him?"
"Instinct", said Out.

Roger, Joan and Michael at Southampton
The boys had just arrived back from the Falklands
On the Canberra

In 1982 April - June we had a very worrying time when Michael and Roger (who both became Royal Marine Commandos) were sent to fight in the Falklands War they both had it bad, Roger was on the Falklands with 42 Commando, they had no proper equipment, and Michael was on the frigate Sir Geraint shooting down Argentine aircraft.

It was a very distressing time for us we would listen to the news on the television, hoping that when we heard bad news about the Falklands that the boys would be ok, the *Lancashire Evening Telegraph* invited people with relatives in the Falklands War to put messages in the paper, John sent messages for the boys we were so very proud of them.

Below are the messages as they appeared in the paper.

PO421OTT, Marine R. P. Eldergill, L Company 4th Troop, Canberra, 42 Royal Marines.

Dear Roger, Hope you are keeping fit and well, and that the weather conditions are not too bad. You have been away now for seven weeks and it seems ages since we saw or heard you, however, everything comes to an end. And please God you will soon be home. All our love, grandma and grandad.

Mr. J. Walsh, 8, Kiln Terrace, Stacksteads.

L/C PL M. Eldergill, PO37881R, 42 Commando RM, Air Defence, Ships Detachment RFA Sir Geraint.

Dear Michael, Hope you are keeping fir and well, and have got your sea legs by now in the rough water of the South Atlantic? We are all praying for your safe return which I hope won't be long now. It will be grand to see you again. All our love, grandma and grandad.

Mr. J. Walsh, 8, Kiln Terrace, Stacksteads.

We all went to Southampton to meet them, it was an extremely hot day the docks were very crowded with excited, expectant, relatives holding banners and waving flags, when the Canberra came into view and blew its loud hooters the noise was deafening it made us jump, but it was such a proud moment, what a relief when the boys finally came ashore, carrying red roses in their teeth, it was a great moment when we spotted Michael and Roger, they were very surprised but thrilled to see us, we hadn't told them we would be there, we had travelled down in a mini bus paid for by the Lancashire Evening Telegraph setting off in the early hours of the morning.

A friend of ours from St Joseph's, Alec Ward was going to Lourdes and I gave him some money to light a candle for the boys, which he very kindly did, he told us it was the last large candle to be lit that day.

Thank God, they both came back safely.

It was an extremely heartbreaking time when Emily our John's wife developed cancer, she was very brave and battled the cancer, but in the end, she became extremely weak and sadly, Emily died. Our John needed our help he was working as a teacher, Christopher his son was just eighteen months old, at the time they lived in Bolton, so John and I used to go down and stay with them, we would look after Christopher in the daytime (he was a very good baby) we really enjoyed being with Christopher and it meant that our John could carry on working. One morning when we were in Bolton, John went for a paper he fell and broke his ankle, and as he could not walk very far so he had to stay at home in Stacksteads. I used to catch three buses to go down to our John's, staying down there during the week and come home at weekends, when I would have to organise things at home for John, men in those days had no idea how to do anything about the home, on one occasion, I had left everything ready for a stew, but John decided to put some barley in the stew, the only trouble was it wasn't barley but rice pudding rice, he ate the stew saying that he had eaten both his dinner and pudding together, goodness knows what it tasted like.

Christmas Day 1983
Me, Christopher, John, and Sally our dog

Looking at the picture above let me introduce you to Sally our dog, Sally was a great dog although born lame she was so intelligent, when John was going to the bookie's she used to get ready and stand by the door, but if we said we were going to church she would lie down on her blanket and roll over for a piece of chocolate, because Sally only walked on three legs, children were always asking John what sort of dog Sally was and he used to reply "a South

African police dog". When we went on holiday, Annie (John's sister) and her husband Bert Lord used to come to stay at our house and look after Sally for us, they looked forward to this, as she was great fun.

Holidays

We went to many lovely places on holiday including Ireland, we really enjoyed going on the musical train, each county we passed through the music from that county would be played, John enjoyed the tour round the Guinness factory and because I didn't drink he had my share of Guinness as well as his own, when we were in Dublin there was a bus strike on everybody was fighting for taxis, we shared a taxi once with some Americans and we let lucky when they paid the fare. We enjoyed having a ride in a Jaunting cart and made friends with a Welsh couple, the two men used to go and watch football while me and the Welsh lady enjoyed looking at the shops everybody was happy.

Enjoying a ride in a jaunting car

We did a tour round Scotland even going up to the Isle of Skye driving through some beautiful countryside, it was a very hot week and we past some lovely spots, when we ask the driver if he would stop so we could enjoy some of the lovely places he drove straight through and said he couldn't stop because the places were not on his schedule, the coach was very comfortable and John was so relaxed he slept all the time on the coach and didn't see a thing. All the hotels we stayed in every night were first class we certainly enjoyed the luxury of staying in the very best hotels.

We also went to Torbay and Paignton, Llandudno and several times to the Isle of Man. In 1973, we were staying in Douglas in the Isle of Man, when there was a huge fire at a place called Summerland (this had been created out of plastic), it was a 50,000 square feet complex which contained restaurants bars and amusement arcades, next door in the Aquadrome were two heated swimming pools a sauna and Turkish bath. Some people from our hotel had asked us to go to Summerland with them, on the very night of the fire, we felt extremely lucky that we had decided against going, many people died in that fire, all night from our hotel window, we could see the thick smoke bellowing out of Summerland it was completely gutted.

When our John and Christopher took us to Spain it was the first time we had been aboard to a hot country, when the plane landed it was evening and quite dark, I remember when I first walked outside off the plane how lovely and warm it felt, stepping out into the night air.

In May 1995, we went to Spain to Benalmadena with Christine to her time-share, it was just when the cup final was about to be played, Everton versus Manchester United, John who had never missed a cup final was not very happy, when he asked the woman in charge at the timeshare, if the football match was going to be on the television and she replied that they needed a special card and unfortunately didn't have one, seeing John's disappointment, she promised she would try to get this card so that John could watch the football match.

On the day of the football match, we went for a stroll along the promenade and John spotted this cafe, which had a board saying that in two hours time the cup final was going to be shown on their TV, John bucked up and decided that he was going to sit and wait for the match to start and settled down on a chair, a couple of English lads Everton supporters were also waiting to watch the match, they said they would keep an eye out for John, we agreed to leave him at the cafe with a cup of tea and strict instructions not to move until Christine came back.

Me at the cafe in Benalmadena waiting to see if John was coming back with us to the timeshare

When Christine and me got back to the time-share, the woman in charge came over to us, very excited saying she had managed to get the card for the cup final so the match was going to be on the TV, we hadn't the heart to tell her John had stayed at the cafe.

John Watching the Cup Final in Spain May 1995

John really enjoyed him-self and luckily Everton won by one goal to nil.

At Easter time our John and Chris would take us out for the day, we always got pleasure out of going to Hollingworth Lake, along with many other people, on the way there we would always be in a traffic jam, Once we were there, we would enjoy a long walk around the lake, and then have a well-earned rest and an Ice cream.

John and Me enjoying a day out at Hollingworth Lake

When Christine went to live in West Sussex, we would go and see her and spend our summer holidays there, sometimes Chris would come with us.

John, Me, Christopher and Christine at Balcombe, West Sussex

Occasionally we would stay in the caravan at West Witterings, this is a lovely little seaside place, we would have a stroll around the village, before walking along the beach and if Chris was with us have a game of cricket on the sands.

John and Me at Witterings

After a good day out we used to enjoy a game of dominos, if I won John used to say I was reneging.

John with Michael and the Old Boneshaker

Once when we were in Balcombe on holiday, Michael wanted to show off this old land rover, he had brought from his friend Danny who lived in Burnley, and take John for a ride around Balcombe, John got into the land rover, but it shook him up so much he was not impressed at all and he couldn't wait to get back to the house.

Every Thursday John went to the Post Office at Stacksteads station, to draw our pensions, one Thursday he was on his way as usual to get the pensions, but as he crossed over the street at Stacksteads railway station, a car knocked him down he was in a really bad state of shock, somebody sent for an ambulance, which took John to Rossendale Hospital, he was very lucky that apart from bruises all over his body his injuries consisted of a broken elbow, I got a big shock when the police came knocking on our door to inform me about the accident.

Just when we thought, John was well enough to come home from hospital, he fell out of bed and landed on his broken elbow, eventually John did come home, but because of the arthritis in my hands social services allocated a team of girls they came to do the washing and to help John wash and dress, Lilly, Janet, and Kath they were all lovely and a Godsend to me.

After this ordeal, we went on holiday to Shanklin in the Isle of Wright with Christine we had a lovely time except for the last day, that unfortunate day we went to Cowes and decided to go on a boat ride round the harbour, while we were walking along the quay going to the boat, John tripped and fell I will never forget the sound of the thud as his jaw hit the ground there was blood and teeth everywhere, sat on a nearby bench there was a man who luckily had a mobile phone, he rang for an ambulance, when it arrived I went in the ambulance with John who was in great pain, Christine followed us in her car.

When we arrived at the hospital we had to wait for a bed, they were very busy, but eventually a bed was found, I have never seen John in so much pain, he was covered in blood and all his teeth had been smashed he was in a right mess, once John had settled down for the night the doctor was very helpful because we needed to find digs, near the hospital, he gave us a list of accommodation and even let us use a hospital phone to enquire if there were any vacancies, it was peak holiday time.

Christine and I had to drive back to the hotel in Shanklin to collect our things we stayed there the night, then in the morning drove to our new digs in Newport we also had to cancel the ferry crossing, when we finally got back to the hospital, John wasn't looking any better and still in lots of pain, then after an x-ray they found he had a broken jaw, all John wanted to do was to go home and kept asking us to bring his clothes, but the doctor said that he wasn't fit to travel, we stayed there in Newport for over a week before finally we got the ferry back to Portsmouth and then onto West Sussex.

John then had to go to Brighton Hospital as an outpatient until it was decided he was fit to travel back home to Stacksteads.

I saw an advertisement in the paper for an apartment to rent in the North of Blackpool at Gyn Square, and then we asked Christine and Christopher if they would like to come with us, we found out you could hire a wheelchair from the Red Cross, so we got one for John it made life a lot easier, Christopher and Christine took turns pushing the wheelchair - John said Christine pushed it far to slow, so Chris took hold of the chair, with John holding on for dear life and ran down the prom with the wheelchair.

We enjoyed sitting in the sun lounge on the North Pier, listening to music being played on the organ, once we sat there enjoying the music soaking up the sun having cups of tea, when all of a sudden smoke started coming up from under a plastic stool that John had his feet on, he had a habit of putting his cigarettes out with his fingers and putting the stumps in his pocket, this time he must have missed his pocket and the cigarette stump had fallen on the wooden planks of the pier floor, we acted quickly Christine and me poured the tea, which we had left in the teacups onto the smoke and put the fire out, but the wooden floor was charred an alarm must have gone off because we saw a few men looking around as though they were searching for something, we just ignored them.

We went to a different place every day, we had a good time in the Tower Ballroom we drank tea and had cakes to eat, while we watched the dancing and reminisced, in the Sea Life Centre, John lost his hearing aid it was very dark in there, so we were very lucky when Christopher managed to find it in the crowds, after an enjoyable walk round Stanley Park we sat in the sun watching Christine and Christopher playing bowls, another day we visited Freeport at Fleetwood, we went in a shop and left John sat outside in his wheelchair, when we came out what a shock he was nowhere in sight we ran round all the shops and eventually found him, it had started to rain so a woman had pushed him in a shop doorway.

On our last night we went to see Hot Ice the Ice Skating Show at the Pleasure Beach, we had good seats because of John in his wheelchair the show was brilliant the costumes and the lighting effects were just spectacular.

This was the last holiday that John and I had together.

24th July 1997 Diamond wedding 60 years married

The Last Years

After the death of Harold Bridge our Margaret's husband, she always came up to our house on Saturday mornings and after lunch we would catch the bus and go to Accrington for a day out roaming around the market and the shops, two years after Harold's death our Margaret died of lung cancer, it was a very painful death and very upsetting for me.

John died on New Year's Eve day 31st December, 1998 in Burnley General Hospital, after we had a been together for nearly 62 years with a lot of ups and downs, one thing he had was a good sense of humour, we always used to have a laugh mostly at ourselves.

I still catch the bus on Saturdays and go to Accrington Market but I am now on my own.

One Sunday shortly after John had died, I went to church with Lorna the wife of my grandson Roger Lorna's mother Evelyn, Jordan and Adam, my great grandsons and our Christine, after mass I went as I always did to light some candles I don't know what happened but somehow the fur hat I was wearing caught fire, Lorna and Evelyn saw what had happened and shouted for somebody to put the fire out, luckily there was a tall young man stood behind me (I had never seen him before) he grabbed my hat off my head and put out the fire. John had never liked that hat.

At 99 years of age, I fell banging my head and breaking my wrist, after being in Fairfield hospital, I have had a short stay in a care home, Greenmeadows in Newchurch (I think this used to be Father Cashell's house where I went after making my first Holy Communion all those years ago) now I have had the plaster removed, I have been allowed to come back to my own home, although my eyesight is failing I had one cataract removed but they found out I have Glaucoma so it hasn't made much difference.

I am now having more attention than I have ever had Lilly, Janet and Kath are looking after me although it is only for six weeks, but it is wonderful to see them again, Sharon used to come and clean for me once a week, after she finished I got Margaret from Bacup to do the cleaning, also Cathy comes from Helmshore and does my hair once a week.

My family are always phoning me and calling in to make sure I am okay, Joan and Roy call on Friday, Joan does a great job of cleaning my kitchen and Roy gets my shopping from the Co-op up Bacup, although I don't think he can always read my writing, Christine comes over on Saturdays we have lunch sometimes a tin of soup or a cheese and onion pie from the bakers down the road and then we go out for the day in her car, every Sunday John and Chris come to pick me up and take me down to their house for a meal and we listen to Irish music.

When Lilly, Janet and Kath stopped coming to see me I got put out for tender and then things started to go wrong, I never knew who was coming or what time. So one Saturday morning our Christine came as usual and decided to take me home with her to stay for a bit, that's why I went to live in Blackpool, I became 100 years old when I lived there and enjoyed a visit from Mary my niece who lived in Australia also Claire and Barry our Jacks daughter and her husband came to see me also Pat Usher who married Gerard Usher my cousin came from Scotland, our Joan and Roy and Carolyn my granddaughter were always coming to take me out and also John and Chris, I got pushed everywhere in my wheelchair. I would have porridge every morning and if the sun was shining sit in the garden, I even got a liking for garlic bread something I had never eaten before, Bernard our Christine's husband is a good cook also he is a good window cleaner, we spent many a happy hour listening to Russell Watson singing, although I really liked to just sit there in peace and quiet.

I am in touch with all my nieces and nephews from all over the world they telephone or write to let me know what is happening in their lives, I have a good family around me: Our John, Joan and her husband Roy, Christine and her husband Bernard, my grandchildren Michael, Roger and his wife Lorna, Carolyn and her husband Garry, Lisa and her husband Thomas and Christopher and Sarah and of course my six great grandsons Ryan and Jordan, Jordan and Adam and the latest addition twins Elliot and Mattheo born to Lisa who lives in Switzerland (our Joan's daughter).

Now everybody from my era all my sisters, brothers aunties, uncles, cousins and friends apart from Annie Whitehead and John's cousin Derek in Grantham and Eileen Bracewell (nee Gordon) John's cousin - Uncle Tom's daughter are dead.

I have seen many changes in my lifetime big changes: travel, motorcars, aeroplanes, space travel, radios, telephones, televisions, decimalisation, credit cards, videos, computers, mobile phones, fridges and freezers people today are cleverer than we were but I don't think they are as happy.

Annie Whitehead my good friend from long ago will be 100 years old in July, just like me she doesn't know why she is still living, the last time I went to see her she made me laugh when she summed it up with Hell's full and God doesn't want me.

One thing I have learnt in life is that everything passes, good or bad nothing stays the same.

18th January 2009

Katie 100 years old and still going strong

A write up from the Rossendale Free Press about Katie's 100th Birthday:

Birthday milestone

Katie Walsh celebrated her 100th birthday with more than thirty-five people family and friends at the weekend.

On Sunday, the great-grandma enjoyed a mass at St. Joseph's Church Stacksteads followed by a party at the Rose 'n' Bowl in Stacksteads.

Present Time

Katie who is 102 years old is now living at Ash Cottage Care Home still with strong memories of her past and her family, which is of great importance to her she loves to be outside especially if the sun is shining, her brain is still active but her eyesight is failing, the one thing that would make a big difference to her would be if she could see, she once asked me if she could go and live back in her own home, I explained that she now gets everything done for her and doesn't need to work anymore her reply was "if you think it is so good here you stay and I will go back to your house".

The sad thing is we have had to sell her home to enable her to stay in care at Ash Cottage.

Nevertheless, she remains the lovely lady she has always been, not wanting to make a fuss and thinking the best of everybody.

Katie sadly passed away on 20th January 2012.

Catherine ('Katie') Walsh neé Hardman

Born 18th January 1909

-

Died 20th January 2012

Printed in Great Britain
by Amazon.co.uk, Ltd.,
Marston Gate.